# Role of Information Technology in Marketing of Household Product

*The findings/views/opinions expressed in this book are solely those of the authors and do not necessarily reflect the views of the editors.*

**Lulu Publication**

# Content

# 1

# Introduction

Information technology has assumed a vital part in marketing research. The business condition of today is complex to the point that no normal chief would need to settle on essential choice without securing enough data. Notwithstanding, it must be noticed that not all snippets of data are pertinent. In marketing research, data gathering must be deliberate and objective keeping in mind the end goal to give an extensive and pertinence data to the analyst. This will help basic leadership. Information technology is the technology that backings exercise including the creation, stockpiling, control and correspondence of data together with their related strategies, management and application. The rate at which Information technology is being created will change the way toward marketing research in India. Be that as it may, the improvement of Information technology will achieve quick change and advancement in marketing research. Data is the life blood of both an individual and association. It is crucial and basic to the development and survival of each association. In marketing, data serves both as an impetus and channel for which the associations' items, managements and thoughts achieved the want goal. The globalization of Information technology has been a huge preferred standpoint to marketing research. Information technology will empower the chiefs, marketing scientists and advertisers to distinguish plainly the marketing issues and openings. Due to

(1) The limit crossing nature of as far as possible, and

(2) Marketing's progress toward a dynamic, developmental process, and organization focused view, exhibiting method has come to be an inside fragment of the association's business rationality.

That is, in a data concentrated, aggressive commercial center, marketing system is in charge of guaranteeing that all parts of a company's marketing exercises are centered around conveying better an incentive than client. Further, perceiving data/learning and IT as possible wellsprings of upper hand, this part investigates different IT-empowered abilities that impact the company's marketing system. In doing as such, particular IT-empowered capacities that compare to Market Orientation Strategy, Relationship Marketing Strategy, Market Segmentation Strategy, and Brand Equity Strategy are shown and inspected. At long last, this part finishes up with a call for purposely orchestrated research for examining, conceptualizing, making, and evaluating IT-engaged limits that effect promoting framework.

Information technology is a term which alludes to the strategies, procedures, and systems that we use in sharing data to different people. This very technology may likewise be utilized with regards to marketing or Advertising a specific item or management. Information technology is helping this industry to enhance its execution by conveying more Sales and benefit to their organizations. The accompanying are a portion of the reasons on why Information technology has helped a considerable measure with regards to marketing a specific item or management. Promotions come in numerous shape and this incorporate online notice, TV plugs, radio advertisements, and even through messages. Relatively every type of correspondence that we have might be utilized to promote an item or an management.

On the web, marketing is path less expensive than Advertising through TVs and other media. This is on the grounds that the web has a more extensive exhibit of gatherings of people from where a publicist could guide the ads to.

With the presence of the web and administration information frameworks (think PCs, phones, and programming), associations have possessed the capacity to change from neighborhood mother and pop shops to worldwide commonly recognized names. To stay aware of rivalry because of web commercialization, organizations are progressively swinging to Information technology (IT) - or equipment, programming, and broadcast communications systems - to streamline managements and lift execution. All things considered, IT has turned into a basic component in the business scene that has helped organizations cut expenses, enhance correspondence, fabricate acknowledgment, and discharge more imaginative and alluring items.

**IT Streamlines Communication**

Productive correspondence is basic to organization achievement. In an inexorably associated and scattered business scene, enlisting, holding, and utilizing representatives requires continuous correspondence and joint effort. A key favorable position of Data innovation lies in its ability to streamline correspondence both inside and remotely. For example, web based assembling and video conferencing stages, for instance, Skype, GoToMeeting, and WebEx allow associations to team up for all intents and purposes progressively, fundamentally lessening costs related with expediting customer's website or speaking with staff who works remotely. Moreover, IT enables associations to interface easily with worldwide providers and buyers.

**IT Facilitates Strategic Thinking**

One of the major points of interest of IT is its capacity to upgrade an organization's upper hand in the commercial center, by encouraging vital reasoning and learning exchange. Getting to and utilizing interpersonal organizations and membership databases, for example, has empowered organizations the capacity to gather, decipher and exchange data more than ever. This has given association's unparalleled access to customers and buyers, engaging relationship to pass on new and upgraded items. Along these lines, when utilized as a key speculation as opposed to as a necessary chore, IT gives associations the instruments they have to legitimately assess the market and to actualize systems required for a decisive edge.

**IT stores valuable information**

The limit, preservation, and support of information - known as information administration - are another space in which IT shimmers. Information administration is essential to any business that must store and shield touchy data, (for example, money related information) for drawn out stretches of time. IT oversees associations the ability to store, offer, and support records for later utilize, and also shielding data from unapproved people. Thus, IT gives organizations the significant serenity that the data they gather and break down can be appropriately put away and defended for some time later.

**IT Cuts Costs and Eliminates Waste**

In spite of the fact that IT might appear to be costly when initially actualized, over the long haul, in any case, it turns out to be unfathomably financially savvy by streamlining an organization's operational and administrative procedures. The usage of online preparing programs is an exemplary case of IT enhancing an association's interior procedures by diminishing expenses and representative time spent outside of work. In reality, IT engages associations to achieve more with less, without surrendering quality or regard.

On the off chance that a publicist just needs to promote a specific item to a gathering of beautifying agents fans, he will just most likely publicize on sites where there are a ton of beautifiers fan guests in this manner additionally limiting the cost of Advertising through the web.

Quick moving buyer products are all the rage. FMCG industry is the most far reaching industry of the world, that arrangements with the generation, bundling, circulation and marketing of shopper merchandise like stationery, dishes, ponder items, House hold items, plastic products, sustenance and dairy items including bundled nourishment items, customer gadgets, equipment and sterile items, and some more. Also the shoppers of FMCG are the populace around the world. With customers slanting towards the technology step by step, it has turned out to be vital for the FMCGs to receive Information technology to come to their focused on gathering of people.

A portion of the very presumed FMCG organizations like Coca Cola, Britannia, Pepsi, L'Oreal, Nestle, and so on, Information technology as a compulsory business supporter and connected it to make things simple for them and in addition clients. The chiefs of FMCG businesses have comprehended that including Information technology is a savvy choice to remain in front of their rivals. The real difficulties that FMCGs confront are growing item portfolio, overseeing Stock keeping units, following field workers, overseeing supply chains and circulation channels, human resource division management including every day wages and finance, meet particular necessity of clients, representatives announcing, guaranteeing consistence with changing business sector patterns, get continuous access to contenders exercises, oversee multi-channel marketing, and some more. With these conceivable complexities FMCG pioneers over all industry verticals understand that IT can assume an amusement changing part that can empower income development by starting advancement and in this way have begun putting resources into the same.

Numerous IT Outsourcing organizations have developed as pioneer in giving Information technology managements to FMCGs as they are likewise all around familiar with the way that buyer is going portable and FMCGs do require their managements to keep pace with the customers. Information technology in FMCG area is as:

**ERP programming:** A venture resource organizer is the thing that a FMCG urgently needs. An ERP system oversees stock system, monitor stock records, deal with various requests, bookkeeping exchanges, and control numerous conveyance channels, production network management, work process management, Logistics management, MIS detailing. No one inquiries the significance of ERP these days. ERPs are presently all around converged with the working of FMCG organizations.

**Portable applications:** The significant worry of FMCGs is to make a brand an incentive for purchasers by serving them at the correct time and opportune place. This is the place Mobility arrangements appear. With versatile applications catching real space in client's Smartphone, they render exceptionally customized understanding. Versatile applications can enable buyer to find your item store calm, surf your item portfolio whenever, get cautions on rebates and offers, buy online from anyplace whenever. Portable applications can enable FMCGs to fabricate client steadfastness.

**Sales Force Automation:** With FMCGs spread over extensive topography, Sales are led by various stores situated in various regions. It is consequently a bad dream for Sales and marketing folks to merge the things. Sales constrain mechanization thus turns into a vital device for FMCG associations. IT organizations can help create Sales drive arrangements that interface customers and providers. Catch and track orders, set targets, track field sales representative, continuous understanding into information, stock management, and so forth are a portion of the highlights of offers drive automation system.

**CRM:** Another supernatural occurrence of Information Technology for FMCGs is Customer Relationship Management and trusts me industry pioneers love CRM. Reason being, CRM help hold profitable clients and if there should arise an occurrence of FMCG CRM is rehearsed at retailers or wholesaler levels. Industry monsters are utilizing CRM to setup client mind focuses, propelling bulletins, giving warnings, and so forth.

So with these advantages of Information technology the FMCGs are quickly disposed towards IT businesses for such arrangements. On the off chance that you have a place with FMCG part and are searching for an IT outsourcing organization then International IT occasions are a decent place to search for.

Information technology drives development and advancement is the way to business achievement. Advancement in business has a similar effect that steam had on the mechanical insurgency.

Truth be told, it's difficult to envision any business that has not profited from the computerized insurgency. Notwithstanding something as involved as agribusiness utilizes PCs. Ranchers utilize PCs for generation records, money related arranging, inquire about on specialized issues, and acquisition.

These days the recipe for business achievement is basic: drive advancement with Information technology. Thusly, the essential thing new organizations in any industry endeavor to understand are the way by which to settle on keen IT enrolling choices. Without a spine of Information innovation, a business wouldn't go far.

We get a kick out of the chance to envision that mankind has dependably been inventive. Be that as it may, development was a gradual undertaking for the greater part of the twentieth century. It was crafted by singular virtuoso or research organizations. Generally, splendid individuals enhanced and the general population gradually embraced the thought. The standard relationship with advancement started with the technology of the PC. It achieved energy with the introduction of the Internet.

In the 1980s, advancement was a bit much for business achievement. A business could do well simply conveying a demonstrated plan of action. Productivity was not a prime order.

Following convention was a sensible method to remain in business. A store proprietor, for instance, was content with utilizing a money enroll like the one imagined by James Ritty in 1879 to keep his legislature from appropriate his cantina remuneration in Ohio, Dayton.

The changes on 6 August 1991 were a small-recollect date, when the WWW went live in world. There was not really a specifies of it in any news study on the planet. A great many people around globe had no clue that the Internet existed. Despite the fact that Tim Berners-Lee's development changed the world as we probably am aware it, it was just toward the finish of the decade that the Internet wound up well known.

**The Rise of Technology**

The ascent of advancement can be followed to humankind getting more astute. As indicated by the Flynn Effect, general IQ has started to ascend since the 1930s. The normal IQ has ascended from 80 focuses to 100 focuses.

While developments in movement and sight and sound enhanced aggregate insight, these were chiefly inactive types of learning. Today, PC applications and the worldwide cerebrum have exchanged on dynamic learning and enhanced how quick individuals learn new things.

**Technology in Business**

Information technology encourages development in business. Development brings about more brilliant applications, enhanced information stockpiling, quicker preparing, and more extensive data dissemination. Development influences organizations to run all the more productively. Furthermore, development builds esteem, upgrades quality, and lifts profitability. Advancement through Information technology has made the accompanying radical changes in business:

- ✓ Online shopping is more effective than shopping in a store.
- ✓ Digital marketing is more effective than high cost newsstudy, TV, and radio Advertising.
- ✓ Social organizing is more productive than going to clubs.
- ✓ VoiP correspondence is more productive than heritage communication.
- ✓ Cloud registering is more proficient than a private PC arrange. Organizations that have grasped the development worldview

have a tendency to have the accompanying attributes:

- They have more precise business arranging
- They have more viable marketing
- They have higher worldwide Sales
- They have more deliberate management

9

- They utilize ongoing observing
- They offer moment client bolster

Truth be told, it's difficult to consider long haul business development without the push of Information technology. Key parts of quickened business development. The innovative transformation has enhanced organizations this century in the accompanying five essential ways:

**Information technology has given business the apparatuses to take care of complex issues**

Enhanced equipment (more memory, speedier processors, more keen visual presentations, and so forth) joined with more intelligent applications (Mindmapping programming like X Mind, shared programming like Kanban sheets, coordinators like Google logbook, and so on) have made it less demanding to explore information, examine it, and plan versatility.

**Information technology enables organizations to settle on better choices**

Great choices in business depend on strong statistical surveying. This should be possible through connecting with groups through video meetings, looking into open assessment via web-based networking media and industry discussions, and utilizing on the web overviews to get client criticism. There are additionally instruments like Microsoft CRM Dynamics and Google Analytics.

**Information technology has enhanced marketing**

Web marketing utilizing internet advertising strategies (SEO, PPC, Facebook Ads) are significantly more precise routes than conventional marketing of discovering target groups of onlookers, finding their necessities, and building a marketing effort to convince them to purchase. It's hard to perceive what number of individuals read a news study promotion. It's anything but difficult to make sense of what number of individuals tapped on an online pennant.

**Information technology has enhanced client bolster**

Clients can get bolster from various stations phone, messages, online networking stages, online classes, et cetera. Moreover, client relationship management systems enable organizations to comprehend client conduct.

**Information technology has enhanced resource management**

Distributed computing enables an organization's representatives to utilize any gadget anyplace on the planet to get to their undertaking level programming.

**Technology is the Wave of the Future**

In the event that the reason for business is to expand benefits, at that point development is the best approach to make more benefits, quicker. The narrative of Jan Koum provides us some insight how much huge organizations esteem advancement. He went from nourishment stamps to extremely rich person as a result of his creation of WhatsApp.

**BACKGROUND OF THE STUDY**

Consistently both small and big organizations discover methods for utilizing technology to give them selves' upper hand. These organizations gadget approaches to bit their rivals through making very much arranged upper hand systems. They endeavour to give a management or an item in a way that client's esteem and this puts them in front of their rivals. Be that as it may, you need to take note of that technology alone won't make you unique and increase upper hand; you should likewise know how to utilize it with the goal that you implement our plans well. Since this expertise is spreading to begin with, everybody can access it, however what will make you diverse is the way you utilize it.

Advertising is the methods for illuminating and in addition affecting the overall population to purchase an item or managements through visual or oral messages. An item or management is promoted to make mindfulness in the brains of potential purchasers through different Advertising mediums, for example, News study, Magazines, Television, Radio, Posters, Hoardings, Billboard and in late time web and web marketing. It is a limited time action for marketing aware. In the present day universe of large scale manufacturing and dissemination, Advertising fills in as a capable apparatus in the marketing procedure. Advertising is utilized for imparting business data to the present and imminent clients. It more often than not gives data about the marketing firm, its item characteristics, place of accessibility and so on.

The term 'Advertising' is gotten from the Latin word 'air conditioning/vertere' which signifies 'to turn' the consideration. Each bit of marketing endeavours to turn the consideration of the perusers or the audience members or the watchers towards an item. The most broadly acknowledged meaning of Advertising is the one which is given by the American Marketing Association, as indicated by which marketing is "any paid type of non-individual introduction and advancement of products, managements and thoughts by a distinguished backers" (Kazmi and Batra, 2008). In any case, the definition has a few restrictions since it doesn't discuss the influence part of Advertising, without which it is extremely hard to accomplish marketing destinations. An overview of late Advertising and marketing reading material makes it clear that there is no all-around acknowledged meaning of Advertising; however certain repeating components, for

12

example, paid, non-individual, distinguished supporters, broad communications, demonstration of influence makes marketing to be controlled methods for mass correspondence, may take any frame visual, oral or written to advance an item through enticing correspondence to accomplish a pre decided targets, changing and fortifying the coveted demeanor of the customers at the purpose of procurement. The Advertising message is considered as an essential part in marketing correspondence process. It is the idea, thought, demeanor, picture, or other data that the promoter wishes to pass on to the intended interest group. How a marketing message is introduced is fundamentally vital in deciding its viability. A perfect marketing message should charge and draw consideration, hold the intrigue, stir want for ownership of the item, and evoke activity.

To profit by technology, you need to get enough preparing or contract an accomplished individual to take every necessary step for you. Most associations they hold marketing workshops to instruct their representatives on the most proficient method to grasp new marketing devices gave by rising technology. It is imperative to stay up with the latest so you lessen on expenses of enlisting experts and increment on generation.

**Utilization of technology in marketing:**

1. Enables organizations to increase upper hand: If an organization figures out how to grasp new technology, it will convey its management and items to its customers first which will fulfil the shopper and acquire confide in that organization. For this situation, when an organization utilizes technology to accelerate its managements or creation, it wins the clients trust subsequently stretching out beyond rivalry. When your rivals

will utilize that innovation as business, we have the best offer of the market.

2.  Utilize innovation to fortify your picture name: A brand name is so basic, if all around cutting edge and it passes on what it says, purchasers will review overlook that brand. Gives take a gander at some noticeable brands a chance to like Coca Cola, Google, Pepsi, Facebook, BBC, CNN, MacDonald, Puma, Nike and some more. Each one of these brands are enormous and they pass on quality. What is clever, a large portion of these best brands are contenders of each other, anyway every one of them has bundles of customers. This rings a toll, that resistance is strong for business, so despite the fact that your organization is still small, continue grasping new developing technologies and give a superior management.

Technology to make a solid brand name: Use interpersonal organizations: After making an extraordinary item, you should assemble a fan base. Individuals who will feel cheerful for that thing and the best place for this is ''Facebook'' Starting at now it has more than 900 million clients, yet every one of these clients has a particular intrigue. So as a business, you should make a business page and advance it focusing on individuals of a particular intrigue. The trap with informal communities is that you need to resuscitate your page with enthralling information that will address your fans, so once every day, Facebook will exhibit these updates by methods for realize minute comes yet rather finished the whole deal; it will end up one of your most noteworthy wellsprings of clients.

The Internet is changing the item and managements accessible bigly. In proficient managements, the Internet is enabling firms to grow new 'bundled' items – now and again by giving coordinated or related managements, for example, monetary and home specialist's managements. Utilizing extranets implies that specific customers can be given access to the association's inward systems which the two includes esteemed and 'secures' customers to our management. The extension of the Internet is making new issues as far as legally binding rights and copyright as well – new management regions for attorneys.

**Price**

The Internet enables a great deal of data to be gotten effortlessly by clients. One reaction is that it is considerably less demanding to look at costs making value rivalry fiercer. The utilization of PC systems to lessen the time and exertion engaged with creating and conveying items and managements implies that providers can either expand their edges or offer similar managements at a lower cost. Commoditization is likewise happening where individuals 'bundle' new items and managements together and offer them, by means of technology, at a lower value (the high volume, low esteem approach). On-line payment (through Visas) makes it more advantageous to customers/clients and can make money accumulation snappier and less expensive for providers – again expanding the likelihood of value diminishments. However the Internet can make it more hard to offer prejudicial estimating (i.e. diverse costs for various client gatherings).

**Place**

The improvements in the energy of databases implies that immediate marketing is extremely going to the fore enabling new fragments to be all the more effectively recognized and enabling sections of-one to be productively focused on. Authorization marketing has been conceived however is still in its earliest stages. The Internet is additionally an incredible wellspring of data – enabling you to stay

15

aware of your rivals' and customers' exercises. On-line surveys and studies can yield a lot of extra data about your customers.

It additionally implies that it is significantly more hard to hold any type of separation when your managements and approach are clear for all – including your rivals – to see. The Internet additionally enables you to achieve a considerably more extensive land spread than was already conceivable. The Internet makes advertises all the more even – enabling smallr players to rival huge players and abroad contenders to enter new markets effortlessly. Some contend that the Internet is simply one more channel which needs overseeing only the same as different channels (e.g. retail outlets, stockrooms, regular postal mail and so forth).

**Promotion**

In pretty much every circle of advancement – marketing, coordinate marketing, individual offering, marketing – CD Roms, sites, personalisation and intelligence are rolling out principal improvements to the way marketing works. For instance:

**Marketing**

You require a site – regardless of whether just as an on-line pamphlet. You have to promote to get movement to your site. You can give a web deliver in notices to give additional data or to catch client data and requests. Computerized TV and the telecom transformation (counting web TV) makes mass Advertising commonsense and reasonable for significantly smaller organizations than beforehand, There are a wide range of new marketing media now accessible – electronic blurbs, data booths, standard ads, on-line index passages and so forth. Association and mixed media are testing the imaginative medicines of advertising too.

**Coordinate marketing**

Database technology lined up with computerized printing of short keeps running of full shading special materials has dramatically affected post office based mail. Email records make it simpler to have more normal and centered correspondences with key clients and customers. The utilization of call focuses and PC helped voice communication are modifying the books on client management and satisfaction. Authorization marketing is the place clients give data about their needs and inclinations and consent to the provider utilizing this data for additionally marketing exercises.

Pamphlets and distributions are presently electronic, intuitive and tailorable to the particular needs and premiums of smallr markets and even people. On the WWW, the client chooses what data they require and in what arrange so some level of provider control is lost. Work area plan and distributing is decreasing the requirement for and cost of costly creators and printers – unfortunately, great outline is getting to be rarer as more novices attempt their hands. Customer correspondence programs are significantly more effortlessly kept up using email and electronic interchanges – which additionally diminishes the cost of postage. Media relations can be upgraded by giving foundation data and news discharges on sites. The Internet condition has created an extensive variety of extra media which are ravenous for good substance.

**Offering**

Those entrusted with offering can utilize the Internet to embrace quick research into prospects. Electronic introductions can be effortlessly custom fitted and exhibited work area side or remotely (by email or video chat). Databases have changed customer and contact management systems and field Sales staff viability and supervision.

**Sales promotions**

The utilization of 3D reproductions and virtual reality implies you never again need to make a genuine presentation space or show suites. Giveaways are regularly technology enhanced (mouse mats, screen savers, free programming and so forth).

McDonald is an example of rundown of impact of technology in marketing: Technology transforms marketing at next step:

✓ Amalgamation – to know our customer

✓ Interactivity – past addressability to exchange

✓ Individualization – data empowered fitting

✓ Independence of area – demise of separation

✓ Intelligence – educated technique

✓ Industry rebuilding – redrawing the marketing map

**STATEMENT OF THE PROBLEM**

The statement of problem is the role of IT in marketing: a study with Reference to House Hold Products Visual pictures assumes an imperative part in catching the consideration of people in general which advances offering of an item through Advertising, where representation and photos are the key mechanism required to communicate the message to an intended group. Yet, these visual components some of the time can't influence the coveted influence because of absence of positive marketing to claim. The Advertising advance is an evaluation to draw some linkage between the items promoted and the goal that is felt by gatherings of people. The choice of reasonable interest is the prime need' for any Advertising that advances an item based on fundamental human wants, needs and thought processes. Regardless of silliness advance being a compelling component for drawing consideration, it is vital for sponsors to locate the suitable apparatus and sort of cleverness to specific things to keep

18

in mind the aim of achievement and brand image. Consideration is improved if the kind of cleverness utilized is specifically identified with the item that is being advanced, in this manner expanding marketing adequacy.

## DEFINITION OF KEY TERMS

Marketing is a hierarchical capacity and resource of procedures for making, conveying and conveying an incentive to clients and for overseeing client connections in ways that advantage the association and its partners.

Data Technology prompted birth of quick and compelling (cost and effect) marketing. Extent of Information Technology in marketing is characterized by the accompanying marketing techniques.

- **CRM**

- **DIGITAL MARKETING**

**CRM**-CRM (Customer relationship management is a term connected to forms executed by an organization to deal with its contact with its clients. CRM programming is utilized to help these procedures, putting away data on present and planned clients. Data in the system can be gotten to and entered by representatives in various divisions, for example, Sales, marketing, client benefit, preparing, proficient advancement, execution management, human resource improvement, and remuneration

CRM isn't only a technology but instead a far reaching, client driven way to deal with an association's theory of managing its clients. This incorporates arrangements and procedures, front-of-house client benefit, worker preparing, marketing, systems and data management. Subsequently, it is imperative that any CRM usage contemplations extend past technology toward the more extensive hierarchical necessities.

19

**Digital Marketing-** it is an act of modernization and management's computerized transference diverts to achieve buyers in a convenient, applicable, individual and practical way. Computerized Marketing Models – Pull versus Push. Computerized Marketing is accomplishing marketing targets through utilization of electronic interchanges technology it is further subcategorized on premise of correspondence channels.

## PURPOSE OF THE STUDY

Marketing experts utilize PC technology to design, oversee and screen crusades. By investigating and controlling information on PCs, they can build the accuracy of marketing efforts, customize client and prospect interchanges, and enhance client relationship management. PC technology additionally makes it less demanding for marketing experts to work together with partners, offices and providers.

- **Enhance Marketing Precision**

With PCs, marketing groups store, dissect and oversee extensive volumes of information on prospects and clients. Understanding the socioeconomics, obtaining histories and item inclinations of various gatherings and people empowers advertisers to target items and battles with more noteworthy accuracy and to customize interchanges.

- **Increment Campaign Capacity**

With cloud resources, advertisers can rapidly build registering limit when they require it. By buying extra processing limit from a cloud specialist organization, as opposed to putting resources into settled systems, advertisers can deal with crests popular. Expanding site ability to deal with extensive quantities of battle reactions, for instance, guarantees that clients don't encounter long holding up times.

Advertisers likewise utilize distributed computing to give the extra ability to test marketing and to oversee huge scale email crusades.

- **Automate Marketing Campaigns**

Marketing computerization is presently a basic component in lead management, the way toward changing over Sales prompts clients. Marketing automation distinguishes a prospect's level of intrigue or goal to purchase in view of the reaction to a progression of messages. The group would then be able to catch up with definite data or a business call, contingent upon the reaction.

- **Open New Communication Channels**

PC technology gives advertisers the chance to construct discourse and reinforce associations with clients and prospects. Advertisers must react to customers' developing utilization of the Internet and online networking. By observing talks on interpersonal organizations and item survey destinations, advertisers can pick up understanding into customer demeanors and accept the open door to react and assemble discourse.

- **Give Efficient Sales Support**

Field Sales groups and wholesalers expect access to marketing bolster material, for example, leaflets, introductions, item information sheets, and Advertising or email formats. By putting away computerized forms of battle material in a safe Web gateway and giving access to approved clients, advertisers can streamline appropriation of help material and increment control over its utilization.

- **Enhance Collaboration**

Utilizing work area video or Web-conferencing apparatuses, advertisers can work together with associates in Sales and item improvement or record groups in marketing offices and marketing consultancies. Coordinated effort apparatuses can speed item advancement by making it simple for groups to meet and take choices, instead of endeavoring to mastermind vis-à-vis gatherings. Office groups can examine or survey battle proposition and changes to guarantee they meet due dates.

**THEORETICAL BASIS**

Information technology (IT) abilities are basic to marketing profession accomplishment in the 21st Century working environment. When you start meeting for marketing positions, you ought to be set up to answer questions particular to your Information technology aptitudes. Now and again, managers may even require possibility for marketing occupations to finish execution appraisals intended to gauge capability in specific sorts of promotions.

**Information technology used in marketing as careers**

Compelling marketing is tied in with getting messages before potential buyers in engaging ways that can possibly impact buy choices. Doing as such in the 21st Century requires the utilization of different Information technology apparatuses. From dealing with your own timetable to staying aware of past contact to dispersing marketing focused data by means of email and online marketing channels, Information technology is instilled in present day marketing employments.

Cases of Information technology devices that marketing experts are probably going to use all the time include:

- Blogging: Many marketing experts are associated with setting up and overseeing web journals for their organizations.
- Computerized Presentations: Marketers are regularly in charge of making electronic Sales and marketing introductions utilizing PowerPoint or different applications.

- Customer Relationship Management (CRM) Systems: Companies regularly utilize refined CRM programming applications to monitor a wide range of client contact, including buying decisions, dissent and only the tip of the iceberg. Advertisers should have the capacity to get to data that is in the system and information extra information as it winds up accessible.

- Email Communication: Marketing experts depend intensely on one-on-one email correspondence so as to achieve their work. Email correspondence is very regular with clients, prospects, colleagues, individual from the media and others.

- Email Marketing: Many organizations depend intensely on email marketing as a method for pulling in new business and building associations with present and past clients. Advertisers are regularly in charge of building and keeping up an email marketing database and also making e-pamphlets and email promotions.

- Graphic Design Software: Marketers who are associated with outlining notices and insurance materials, for example, leaflets and pamphlets, for their organizations are relied upon to be knowledgeable in the utilization of visual communication programming applications like InDesign, PhotoShop and that's only the tip of the iceberg.

- Websites: Having website composition, improvement upkeep aptitudes can be favorable position for people who need to work in marketing. The level of web ability important differs starting with one organization then onto the next. In a few associations, marketing experts are relied upon to deal with each part of making a site, including configuration, programming, security, content improvement and the tip of iceberg. In different associations, marketing representatives work intimately with in-house software engineers or an outside web improvement firm on the specialized parts of webpage management.

- Social Media: With such a large number of organizations consolidating long range interpersonal communication into their special endeavors, marketing experts should be knowledgeable in the utilization of famous online networking promotions as instruments for drawing in new business and building client connections. Advertisers are regularly in charge of setting up and overseeing Facebook pages and Twitter represents their organizations, distributing video substance to YouTube, and building up LinkedIn profiles for key organization work force.

**Planning for Marketing Career Success**

Turning into a fruitful marketing proficient starts with ensuring that you have the learning and aptitudes essentially to adequately elevate your organization to potential clients inside its intended interest groups. This implies you need a working learning about marketing hypothesis as standards and in addition a strong comprehension of how is Information technology utilized as a part of marketing professions. On the off chance that you don't have the IT abilities that are important to meet all requirements for the sorts of occupations you would like to be contracted for, it's dependent upon you to get the preparation important to demonstrate your incentive to planned businesses.

Advancement is the significant technique to achievement in this mechanized age. The method for headway in business infers achieving something different, more brilliant or on the other hand better that will have a valuable result similar to regard, quality or effectiveness by using rising or showed advances of the world. The innovation which has viably substantiated itself in latest two decades is clearly the Information innovation (IT). It has definitely changed the lives of the general population and affiliations. At the present time web based shopping, electronic promoting, person to person correspondence, propelled correspondence and dispersed figuring et cetera are the best instances of advance which got past the deluge of Information technology, Now precise business arranging, powerful marketing, worldwide Sales, orderly management, constant watching, minute customer reinforce and whole deal business improvement can't be proficient at the perfect level without IT.

- **Essentialness of IT in business:**

The accomplishment of every business depends upon particular segments. Some of which are correct examination, picking the right innovation and the future vision. Research from the latest two decade has shown that those affiliations that do place assets into innovation and pick the method for advancement augment their bit of the general business, budgetary figures and general forcefulness. Data innovation is the fundamental innovation which offers you the opportunity to reprieve down specific data and plan your business go as requirements be. It also gives you various mechanical assemblies which can deal with complex issues and plan the flexibility (future improvement) of your business. In the bleeding edge age, it is exhibited that best in class advertising is a remarkable instrument which let you propel your things or administrations to the overall marketplace while sitting in the console of business office. In addition, because of the conveyed figuring and present day correspondence which enable you to outline an overall affiliation, regulate and screen its virtual working environments wherever all through the world. By and by I will rapidly clear up how Information innovation expects a key part in different times of business.

- **Decision Making**

Speed and precision are at the center of settling on right decision for your business. Each productive affiliation needs to encounter an entire factual looking over process which enables administration to settle on the right decision. Factual studying ought to be conceivable from various perspectives through online diagrams, social events, and sites, gather exchanges using World Wide Web and clearly through in-person meets too. Starting at now Big data, Google Analytics and Microsoft CRM Dynamics are also mind boggling mechanical assemblies to isolate accommodating information which can influence on essential administration. These online instruments not simply give consistent responses from the potential social occasion of individuals yet likewise ensure the accuracy of data by restricting the risk of human botches.

- **Marketing and Business Growth**

The center of the business accomplishment lies in its showcasing which enables the administration to recognize its proposed intrigue gather first and thereafter watch their examples and requirements. The general promoting covers open association, Advertising, progression and Sales which along these lines influence on business advancement. Various sorts of showcasing can empower you to accomplish your potential customers. In any case, I will rapidly clear up cutting edge advertising here which was the dream in the past without Internet innovation. Propelled Marketing is a bleeding edge ponders which let you propel your things or administrations wherever all through the world. It is a far reaching term which consolidates various thoughts like site change (SEO), pay per click (PPC), blogging, talk dialog, email shot, SMS, MMS, online informal communication promoting and Smartphone application business et cetera. By and by web exhibit is impacting at a fast pace in light of the way that most of the business visionaries have grasped that the whole deal accomplishment in business isn't possible without mechanized proximity on the web. An enormous number of new destinations are being incorporated the web every year.

- **Customer Support and Satisfaction**

    More elevated amount of consumer loyalty is the way to progress which can't be accomplished without a constant client bolster process. Business attainment relies upon to know about customer's need, training and fulfillment. Successful correspondence is the best device to comprehend the client requests, issues and their answers. On account of the Internet Technology that has empowered us to speak with a huge number of potential or existing client in the ongoing. IT furnishes numerous channels to speak with the client without going out in snow or rain. Some of these channels are email, online course, web-based social networking, part gateways, online pamphlets and content or interactive media informing through latest mobile technology. Endeavor associations regularly utilize client relationship management systems (CRM) to hold important information for understanding client practices and future needs.

- **Resource Management and Globalization**

    Resource management assumes a pivotal part in business achievement. With regards to medium or extensive association, it is hard for the best management to deal with every one of the resources physically. These resources may incorporate unmistakable, money related or HR and so on. Data innovation has accepted a key part in mechanizing such complex issues by introducing simple to utilize courses of action. 10 years back, by far most of the asset administration game plans were work zone based. By virtue of the web and cloud innovation which enables programming architects to display cloud based ERP (Enterprise Resource Planning) courses of action. By and by, the executives can direct or screen their progressive assets in every way that really matters wherever on the planet by using their PC, workstations, tablets or Smartphone. This thought has introduced the likelihood of globalization. Most by far of multinational associations (Microsoft, Google, Amazon, McDonalds et cetera) on the planet use these cloud based responses for manage their virtual or physical work environments and staff far and wide.

# Chapter-2

# Similar Study

**2**

Electronic Marketing industry in India is spread to all the business regions. A fragment of the uses of E-Marketing are shopping and demand following, web based saving money, installment frameworks and substance administration.

The vitality of advanced promoting empowers geophysical obstacles to vanish at whatever point.

Modern industrial concepts in India are impacting Indian market having an amazingly liberal impact on advertising and notice. The 10,000 foot perspective advanced promoting estimations isn't made.

**1996:** B2B(India MART) set up in India.

**2007:** Flipkart was set up in India. Each E-promoting or business endeavors use fundamentally computerized implies for their showcasing purposes.

In 2011, the advanced showcasing bits of knowledge revealed that advertising by methods for the telephone and tablets was 200% lower than that of the next years. In the midst of this current year, the aggregate assets were mind boggling improvement openings and standard advancement determination computerized advertising.

Today, computerized showcasing industry in India is creating at its zenith, is so far constant. Various components are accountable dependable game plan on the web, the underneath figure shows the advanced promoting bits of knowledge.

The conviction pieces of clothing.. This is a direct result of the expect that has been re-built up correspondence organizations. Insignificant exertion of handset is at present open in the end makes a charming business opportunity to pitch to a creating people.

Likewise the progression in the advanced advertising like manner promoting required a stimulating soul constantly.

A couple of parts have been found to add to the improvement of advanced advertising in India. Before now, web use was inferred for the well-off. There is by and by a fantastic 34% of the associations starting at now had a planned computerized showcasing approach in 2016 72% publicists assume that standard model of promoting is never again satisfactory and this will make the association wage to be extended by 30% preceding the complete of 2017.

In 2017, 80% associations will extend their advanced promoting spending which may beat the IT spending design. Simply the uneducated individuals couldn't get to the potential outcomes of the advanced promoting because of the accessibility to enrolling contraptions and PC direction. A substantial number of the overall public accepting a dynamic part in the change of advanced advertising industry in India.

**Portable Marketing**

Advanced promoting survey advertising Consistently, it has been seen that 92% of online long range informal communication customers are from the phones. This engages the degree of computerized showcasing ventures.

**Email Marketing**

Email promoters of without a doubt the best advertising associations affirm a landing best strategies for ensuring changes in 2017. As showed up from the figure underneath, email is a champion among the best techniques for advanced promoting as there is an office to administer messages to countless immediately.

**SEO(search engine optimization) Marketing**

The changes is an existing web crawlers, promoters are moreover endeavoring their strategies for intent on social affair of individuals keeping in mind the end goal to get together with the present progression computerized showcasing happens, practices web based systems administration, email, content, web record, et cetera, advanced promoting genius advanced promoting workplaces or given to specialists.

**Web chutney**

**India's driving computerized promoting association. Web chutney incorporates** detailed key improvements inside authority activity across finished forming more grounded fundamental advanced association in 2008, 2009 and 2011. site structure, flexible congeniality, showcasing, request improvement, viral accounts, Facebook campaigns, Twitter revives, progressing tuning in

➢ **OBBSERV**

Observe is a primary innovation driven computerized promoting and web assets change association set up fiscally sagacious advertising techniques to giving tractable routine with respect to softening statures. Taking everything into account, it's the inventive sentiment doing the study's and immaculate.

**Gozoop**

A standard advanced association other than the prominent administrations like electronic long range informal communication commitment courses of action. Gozoop has an adaptable division too that makes convenient applications. Gozoop administrations are by and by well-known every single through Indium.

31

> **Avignyata Inc.**

Electronic interpersonal interaction showcasing endeavors look for fights and regulate electronic long range interpersonal communication advertising in India. They are one of the pioneer and driving computerized showcasing organizations in Mumbai with skilled specialists with promoting bits of information. They will probably develop a virtual inescapability for the brands, join each one of the zones that decidedly influence the brand, empower clients to research

**BC Web Wise**

This association has really locked in with OK amounts going with administrations: web media plans, destinations, web showcasing, e-releases, compact advertising, online research, content administration. Most of the associations are up 'til now advanced promoting. Smallr urban groups in India are delivering advanced promoting associations. Corporate affiliations exactly when the essential present day PC was envisioned, near around six around the globe. This shows Information innovation can outperform all wants when it creates. Regardless, an "insipid term consolidating an extent of technologys to get, store, process and transmit information". It consolidates the three essential innovation social events of gear, programming and media interchanges. In this way, IT joins PCs, web, videotext, PDAs, advanced trades, individual computerized teammates (PDA) and some more.

> **Email**

Email offers associations a "snappy, versatile and convincing strategy for getting promoting messages through". Half of the UK's masses starting at now has a mail account. This station is all in all less intrusive stood out from telephone promoting. It furthermore gives the decision to interface In any case, sponsors need to manage this

32

instrument with alarm concerning the association's reputation for being customers are starting at now went up against by unconstrained sends. To instruct the customer through email secures in every way that really matters no costs, which is one of its most basic favorable circumstances.

➢ **Broadband**

Broadband portrays a "high point of confinement data transmission framework." Jessica Keyes (2009): Characterized by lightning smart progression, sudden moves in innovation, and shorter lifecycles, its promoting things and administrations demonstrates an exceptional game plan of challenges and frequently requires IT administrators and fashioners to get drew in with the showcasing method. Showcasing IT Products and Services is made to help possessed IT executives and advertising boss get up to speed quickly and easily on what's relied upon to make convincing promoting systems and fights. Focusing on the exceptional issues incorporated, this one-stop asset gives everything anticipated that would understand the parts, commitments, and administration frameworks principal for the headway of successful techniques. It covers key market orchestrating, concentrating on business areas, looking at business sectors, understanding the restriction, fusing business sector and Sales systems, nuances of overall markets, making showcasing spending designs, evaluating, and executing promoting endeavors. An a lot of indeces included on the book's CD empowers you to get up and fleeing. Beside an aggregate advertising glossary, two complete the process of showcasing plans—one for a gear thing; the other for an item thing—engage you to evade the "scut" work of working up a promoting plan so you can base on the creative parts of advertising. Since a showcasing configuration is immovably agreed with an affiliation's business and

33

key plans, this book outfits you with designs for both of these, and furthermore an arrangement for that to a great degree basic methodology for progress official summary. The CD moreover incorporates piles of fill-in designs including customer and contender examination audits, test open articulations, letters of comprehension. In case you have a showcasing need, this book has an intense design to address that issue.

**Jessica Keyes (2016):** Provides cases, case narratives, and stream investigate for fundamental business issues are, for instance, execution estimation and administration, relentless process change, learning administration, peril administration, benchmarking, estimations assurance, and person's administration. It gives IT directors frameworks for improving IT execution and passing on regard, notwithstanding it controls them in picking the right estimations for their IT affiliations. Moreover, it offers learning administration methods to build up an affiliation, shows to supervise perils to abuse openings and plan for risks, and uncovers how to standard an IT affiliation's execution and measure its change. Including 10 segments notwithstanding reference segments, the book begins with a survey of execution based indispensable organizing, after which it analyzes the progression of a quality change (QI) plan, developing benchmarks, and evaluating execution redesigns. It covers how to diagram IT-specific measures and cash related estimations and what's more the establishment of an item estimation program. Starting there, it goes before forward to arranging people change frameworks and discusses such subjects as activity, motivation, selection, and agent examination. The last couple of parts exhibit to use balanced scorecards to manage and measure data based social eager and to perceive, explore, and avoid threats. Despite covering new methods and estimations for evaluating

34

and upgrading IT frames, the maker looks for assessing thing change and executing reliable improvement. The last part considers customer regard frameworks and reveals how to use force field examination to tune in to customers with the goal of improving buyer steadfastness and operational significance.

**Venkatesh(2009):** The accomplishment of a thing or administration depends as much on its showcasing as its make. Likewise, compelling advertising lays on a consistent method to manage the entire innovation cycle, improvement, and zone learning of the promoting work drive. Since Information innovation industry changes speedier than some other industry, vendors and publicists need to stay one next to the other of the latest examples in mechanical change and more breakthrough strategies for passing on IT benefits. A refined record of the author's immediate association with IT, this book intends to give the learning of advertising of IT. Accepting a helpful approach and dialect free vernacular, it clears up how an IT item can be made market-focused at each stage- - from thought to post-Sales reinforce - thusly improving the probability of its accomplishment in the market. Showcasing of Information Technology covers: Introduction to its fundamental item thoughts, things, administrations and authorized innovation rights. Cost and assessing of IT items, and "free and open" items.

**Ashfaque Ahmed (2016):** To develop tried and true, industry-material programming things, far reaching scale programming study packs ought to reliably upgrade programming planning techniques to extend thing quality, support cost diminishments, and stick to tight timetables. Focusing on the fundamental fragments of productive far reaching scale programming studys, Software Study Management: A Process-Driven Approach discusses HR, programming building, and innovation to a level that outperforms most school level courses in regards to the issue, the book is made into five segments, A running relevant examination gives authoritative learning and insider information on the instruments and strategies required to ensure thing quality, diminish costs, and meet examination due dates. This book demonstrates all parts of present day mull over administration sharpen consolidates a plenitude of significant worth configurations that masters can use to amass their own specific instruments. So also important to understudies and specialists alike.

# WHY INTERNET MARKETING IS IMPORTANT FOR BUSINESS?

With respect to the achievement of your business, web showcasing accept a key part. To feature yourself and to propel your things and administrations, you require the assistance of web advertising. If you are expecting to start a business or you are on the way and need to improve your business you can obtain a web based promoting association which Sales with all activities from arranging the website for your business to executing distinctive showcasing systems including Internet advertising. Web promoting will empower you in upgrading your business to check detectable quality, development and Sales. The accompanying are the fundamental 5 reasons why web advertising is basic for your business.

- **To increase the detectable quality of your business**

These days everything ought to be conceivable online from obtaining film tickets to acquiring furniture for home. Web has become enormous changes our lifestyle. Every business should see this and develop their quality on the web. Web advertising is valuable for each one of the sorts of associations. This will empower you to develop your detectable quality to greater masses.

36

- **To interface with the customers**

    Internet organizing advertising empowers you to connect with your potential and returning customers. Revive your customers with the new or latest features of your business. You can plug the best in class things or administrations and give a little depiction of these awesome and administrations to your customers. By doing this you can pull in new customers later on.

- **To adjust up to the resistance**

    These days' family can access and purchase a broad assortment of items from online with the help of web. It is to a great degree basic for any business to keep up the restriction against the little, close-by and far reaching on the web retailers and associations. This is possible exactly when the associations make suitable usage of the web showcasing stage.

- **It is helpful for creative work**

    You can investigate incredible catchphrases which suits your business. You can make use of these watchwords in your business to put your webpage on the most astounding purpose of the web crawler comes to fruition. Proper catchphrase usage empowers you to drive potential action to your site. this is the best way to deal with win new customers.

- **Legitimate yourself**

    By working up and keeping up the closeness on the web, business can demonstrate their clients that their business is dynamic, dynamic and trying to improve and is attempting to create. The Internet empowers neighborhood associations to genuine themselves as productive associations. By this they will have the ability to win and hold a broad customer base. These days computerized cells have ended up being outstanding along these lines, consider a direct application diagram which downloads and keep the business at the forefront of the brains of people.

**COMPUTERIZED MARKETING INDUSTRY IN INDIA**

The vitality of computerized promoting empowers geophysical obstructions to vanish at whatever point, Computerized showcasing having an uncommonly noteworthy impact on promoting and business. The all-inclusive strategy computerized advertising estimations isn't made.

In the region of 1971 and 1972, The ARPANET is used to sort out an arrangement

In 2011, the computerized promoting estimations revealed that showcasing by methods for In the midst of this current year, the aggregate assets were

- 34% of the associations starting at now had a consolidated computerized promoting system in 2016

- 72% publicists assume that traditional model of showcasing isn't any more satisfactory and this will make the association salary to be extended by 30% preceding the complete of 2017

- In 2017, 80% associations will grow their advanced showcasing spending which may beat the IT spending design. Simply the untalented individuals couldn't get to the conceivable outcomes of the advanced showcasing because of the receptiveness to handling contraptions and PC guideline. A significant part of the overall public Adaptable Marketing

Computerized advertising outline promoting. Consistently, it has been seen that 92% of web based systems administration customers are from the PDAs. This enables the traverse of computerized showcasing wanders.

**Email Marketing**

Productive advertising associations declare a landing best technique for ensuring changes in 2017. As showed up from the figure underneath, email is a champion among the best techniques for computerized advertising as there is an office to apportion messages to different people directly.

**Search and SEO Marketing**

Like manner endeavoring shift their strategies for concentrating on gathering of spectators keeping in mind the end goal to get together with the present advancement computerized advertising happens, practices web based systems administration, email, content, web searcher, et cetera. Advanced promoting genius computerized promoting workplaces or given to guides.

**Web chutney:**

India's driving advanced showcasing office. Web chutney incorporates announced key advancements inside authority administration transversely finished assembling more grounded primary computerized office in 2008, 2009 and 2011. The improvement implies the rate of advancement of computerized advertising ventures in India.

**Ashfaque Ahmed (2009):** In the present unforgiving business condition where customers ask for zero defect programming at cut down costs it is attempting that allows to programming associations to seclude them from the restriction. Giving another perspective on this unyieldingly basic limit, Software Testing as a Service clears up, in direct tongue, how to use programming testing to upgrade effectiveness, decrease time to exhibit, and reduce costly oversights. The book clears up how the run of the mill components of amassing can be associated with commoditize the item testing administration to

39

achieve relentless quality over all item studys. This dynamic reference reviews various programming testing gadgets, frameworks, and sharpens and gives brief bearing on the most ideal approach to assess costs, circulate assets, and make centered offers. Packed with cases and case chronicles, this book demonstrates programming change bosses, programming analyzers, testing boss, and business visionaries how genuine orchestrating can provoke the generation of programming that winds up being head and shoulders over the resistance.

**Dr. MahabirNarwal Dr. GeetaSachdeva (2013):** taking care of, securing, transmitting, tolerating, and recouping information. Recollecting its distinctive points of interest, in the present examination an undertaking has been had to analyze its impact on purchaser purchase direct. The disclosures include that IT influences purchaser purchase lead. It is fought that the consequence of the examination will emphatically be valuable for the sponsors to portray their advertising frameworks in like way.

**Vincent K. Omachonu; Norman G. Einspruch(2010):** The human administrations industry has experienced an extension of advancements went for enhancing future, individual fulfillment, scientific and treatment decisions, and moreover the capability and cost reasonability of the social protection framework. Data innovation has accepted a basic part in the headway of human administrations frameworks. Notwithstanding the surge in headway, theoretical research on the craftsmanship and investigation of social protection advancement has been limited. One of the principle driving forces in investigate is a connected framework that outfits researchers with the foundation whereupon their examinations are amassed. This examination begins with an importance of therapeutic administrations improvement and an appreciation of how headway occurs in social

40

protection. A connected framework is then made which verbalizes the intervening elements that drive headway in social protection. In perspective of the proposed importance of social protection improvement, the estimations of therapeutic administrations headway, the methodology of human administrations progression and the sensible framework, this examination opens the passage for researchers to address a couple of request as for progression in human administrations. If the possibility of therapeutic administrations improvement can be lit up, by then it may wind up less requesting for prosperity policymakers and authorities to survey grasp and secure administrations in ways that sensibly see, desire and offer need to really critical human administrations advancements. At last, this examination presents 10 investigate questions that are applicable to the field of human administrations advancement. It is assumed that the reactions to these and other such request will hold the best approach to future advances in restorative administrations improvement analyze.

**Abah Joshua and; Achimugu Philip (2011):** Information innovation (IT) has transformed into a key segment in money related change and a spine of learning based economies to the extent errands, quality transport of administrations and benefit of administrations. In like manner, abusing information propels (IT) is a growing test for making countries. There is by and by creating verification that Knowledge driven progression is an indisputable factor in the power of nations, undertakings, affiliations and firms. Affiliations like the dealing with a record portion has benefitted liberally from e-keeping cash, which is one among the IT applications for fortifying the forcefulness. This examination presents the present example in its utilization in the saving money undertakings in India and gives information into how quality keeping cash has been redesigned by

41

methods for IT. The examination moreover reveals that the association of IT workplaces in the Indian Banking industry has accomplished fundamental changes in the substance and nature of keeping cash business in the country. This examination and enlightenment of how Indian Banks have used IT to reengineer their exercises is positive through composing review and observation. Three groupings of components that relate to the use and utilization of Information innovation devices were considered in this examination. These fuse the nature and level of gathering of inventive innovations; level of utilization of the recognized advances; and the impact of its appointment contraptions on the bank errands.

**Kaylene C. Williams; Robert A. Page (2012):** Each age has outstanding wants, experiences, generational history, and lifestyles, characteristics, and economics that effect their obtaining rehearses. In like way, various associations are interfacing with multi-generational clients and attempting to grasp and get the thought of these different buyers. Multi-generational showcasing is the demonstration of connecting with the exceptional needs and practices of individuals inside more than one specific generational social event, with an age being a get-together of individuals imagined and living about a comparable time. The inspiration driving this examination is to portray rapidly the U.S. ages the extent that the conditions in which they grew up and what's more the characteristics, lifestyles, and mindsets of the social occasion. In any case, the basic point of convergence of the examination is to depict distinctive promoting understandings and procedures appropriate to each age's characteristics and practices, particularly in regards to division, things and administrations, and correspondence. **Ahmad Adel Mostafa (2017):** This examination points out the suitability of thing codes especially energetic response

42

(QR) codes and institutionalized labels in the promoting field. With all the learning and mechanical advancements that the 21st century accomplished, the investigation examines new thoughts that can be considered remembering the ultimate objective to have a beneficial showcasing framework, This investigation is detached into five segments; the essential fragment contains a short preamble to the thing code framework and how it capacities. In the going with fragment, composing review points out how common and unmistakable QR codes and institutionalized labels ended up being nowadays. By then, gatherings and studies are considered in the examination's framework. Next, some explanatory points of interest are familiar with prompt how supportive thing codes are in the promoting an area. Finally, the conclusion supports why this examination should be pondered.

**Karakaya (2001):** The methods by which they survey website characteristics and what impacts them to remain on the destinations.

**Roche, (1992):** In the past two decades, we have seen a passionate addition in the estimation of Information innovation (IT) to business affiliations. Refined, new Information technologies have been a force for some business areas for stock and ventures twisting up extremely worldwide in nature. IT expects a basic part in the coordination of inventive work, age, and advertising practices across finished edges.

**Ives and Jarvenpaa, 1991; Jarvenpaa and Ives, (1993):** The globalization of business areas and undertakings and its changing part inside business affiliations have made its key use a key segment in choosing the achievement of an association their records from any geographic zone they require. The administration information frameworks (MIS) composing is rich in contemplates on its usage as a forceful "weapon" These examinations show that IT plays a basic, if not basic, part in the arrangement of a family organization. Meanwhile, mulls over in the overall administration composing have explored the indispensable forces affecting overall competition, and have shown the differences among these and the engaged forces looked by private associations.

**Senior individuals and Ricks, (1991):** It has all the earmarks of being, regardless, that both the MIS and the general administration composing have, all things considered, ignored IT as a facilitator for expanding high ground in the worldwide field. Furthermore analyze is required on how innovation drives an overall affiliation's structure and method.

Directing advertising information by techniques for IT has ended up being a champion among the most key parts of effective showcasing. By social affair and sharing showcasing information and by using it to progress corporate and mark picture, IS offer better methodologies for improving inward efficiencies of the firm. Information frameworks allow dynamic showcasing correspondence between work drive in corporate orchestrating, accounting, Advertising and Sales progression, thing administration, channels of appointment and direct Sales. Data innovation based promoting information frameworks (MkIS) have been with us for quite a while. The noteworthiness of PCs in showcasing was included by Kotler. For the most part, MkIS has been seen as a framework to help advertising administration in its fundamental initiative. Despite the administration perspective, MkIS can be a crucial instrument for the entire showcasing affiliation. A couple of experts have assembled IS in advertising by the assignments for which they are generally used. Moriarty and Swartz proposed a thought of promoting and Sales effectiveness (MSP)

44

frameworks which includes four subsystems: sales representative benefit instruments, standard mail, telemarketing and Sales administration. In any case, these new, more operational, IS have not yet been used as a piece of the setting of the MkIS thought. With the ascent of web business and spread of e-administration in the country new open entryways are required to be hurled open. E-administration can change the way dealings between people, affiliations and the lawmaking body are endeavored. It will announce ascent of 'e-individual' and 'e-society' which will change the overall population into data based society. E-administrations will be a bit of step by step life and a demand on relationship to meet these essentials would develop.

# Chapter – 3

# Study Procedure

**3**

The customary approach of survey family/ mind the end goal to build up an important examination of this relationship one must go past unimportant appropriation and look at the whole procedure comprising of reception as well as the examples of utilization and in addition the effect of technology on House hold flow.

Digital Strategy is tied in with working out where your home care mark sits in the online world, choosing who you need to reach, and making sense of the most ideal approach to contacting them. It's tied in with keeping up an online nearness to an applicable gathering of people and keeping them locked in. There's no point having a gigantic online nearness if your group of onlookers finds that nearness tedious or irritating. There's a scope of strategies to approach building up a digital technique, and the approach should be custom fitted to fit every specialty. Content Marketing includes making and scattering rich, applicable substance, keeping in mind the end goal to draw in and keep up a characterized gathering of people, and eventually change over this engagement into gainful outcomes. Content Marketing is the specialty of speaking with clients without offering – as opposed to pitching items and managements, home care brands give data that enhances the group of onlookers, e.g. expanding their insight or influences them to grin/snicker. The straightforward thought behind this is if organizations reliably convey significant substance to clients, they will be compensated with clients and dependability.

Most sites with progress are charging for their managements. Yet, there are normally constantly free destinations with nearly a similar item as well as management as the fruitful ones. The group conduct enables a few locales to charge due to the quantity of clients, and others (as a rule in their startup) must remain for nothing out of pocket. Locales have in some cases began their payment design too soon (without enough guests or acknowledgment) and thusly lose the guests to different destinations. Straightforward cases are dating locales. While there are numerous fruitful ones, an extensive number start up each year, and some make it, while others shut down once more.

> **Why think about technique?**

The principle thought of the methodological part is to feature the strategy used to take care of an issue. To do as such, the way one will view and handle an issue relies upon his/her principal presumptions, at the end of the day his/her own impression of reality. At the point when a gathering of individuals cooperates, regularly their impression of reality and, subsequently, of the intricate details of the issue will contrast, coherently, they will concoct unmistakable techniques to address the issue. Consequently, it is important to concede to one single methodological approach keeping in mind the end goal to make a typical comprehension of reality. Such a reception will prompt a characteristic determination of a few arrangements of instruments (worldview, show, and so on.), associated with the picked approach. Adopting up a specific methodological strategy additionally gives a casing for how to function all through the investigation, so the information gathering, its examination, lastly the conclusions drawn out of them is altogether controlled by the decision of these strategies.

> **Relating standards to the methodological methodologies**

When discussing system, there are distinctive ideal models that lie underneath the decision of the three methodologies. As the procedure in each approach separates, it is important to delineate how the four segments of a worldview are seen so as to consolidate the six sociology ideal models to the three methodologies. The origination of reality and science, the logical beliefs and the moral and aesthetical perspectives are to be depicted, as per the approach of systematic, systems methodological perspectives. The accompanying figure goes for giving the peruser a diagram to what degree sociology, orientalise standards and the three methodological methodologies are corresponded.

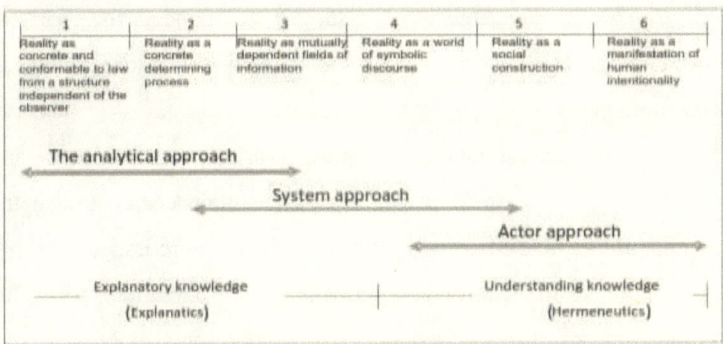

Figure 1: approaches to the six paradigms (Arbnor & Bjerke, 1997)

The Internet is the most focused market ever. Clients tend to bounce to another site on the off chance that they are not inspired by paying for the managements. Most destinations lose a large portion of their guests while presenting payment.

**STATEMENT OF PROBLEM:**

Marketing is a societal procedure, which observes shopper's needs, concentrating on an item or management to satisfy those needs, endeavoring to shape the customers toward the items or managements advertised. In fact, marketing is central to any organizations development. The marketing groups (advertisers) are entrusted to make buyer consciousness of the items or managements through marketing methods. Unless it gives careful consideration to its items and managements and buyers' socioeconomics and wants, a business won't for the most part succeed after some time.

Basically, marketing is the way toward making or guiding an association to be effective in offering an item or management that individuals want, as well as will purchase. Along these lines great marketing must have the capacity to make a "suggestion" or set of advantages for the end-client that conveys an incentive through items or managements.

The announcement of issue is to ponder the part of Information technology in marketing: an investigation with reference to house hold items.

This investigation requires various definitions and delimitations with a specific end goal to maintain center around the essential angles, and to abstain from bringing up more issues. Besides, it is imperative that the diverse terms/ideas that we allude to in this examination are characterized, to give the peruser a more extensive point of view of the issue that we are managing.

One term should be clarified however; popular marketing, which is an idea that have created with the development of the Internet. Viral marketing spreads through social relations, and is viewed as an digital rendition of verbal marketing. Regardless of whether entertaining, astonishing or with profound effect numerous small messages, pictures or even recordings are sent starting with one client then onto the next for different reasons.

## OBJECTIVE OF THE STUDY

The universally useful of the examination is to look at the part of Information technology in house hold items. The magnificence of good substance marketing is that it continues conveying. Rich, important substance doesn't quit being great, thus it can keep on driving business long after it's distributed. Though of our home couldn't care less organization customers, Content Marketing assumes a key part in their digital methodology. Site design improvement SEO remains for "site improvement." It is the way toward getting activity from the "free," "natural," "publication" or "normal" query items on web crawlers. Payment isn't required, as it is with paid pursuit promotions.

Indeed, even before the Internet there were a wide range of approaches to publicize, in various media, for example, radio, TV, news study's, magazines, and also by means of telemarketing or handouts. Normally the objective was to get an organization or potentially item name, an announcement and so on conveyed to whatever number individuals as could be expected under the circumstances at the smallest cost conceivable.

At the point when the Internet emerged, various pursuit choices ended up accessible. Organizations had the choice to publicize themselves on a bigger scale. Because of Advertising discernment at the time, numerous organizations were accepted to have incredible esteem, and in this manner exchanged on the stock trade at unprecedented high rates. The Internet was relatively dismissed in light of numerous fizzling site based organizations that had desires to the market and suspicions about purchasers. In any case, the two customers and organizations kept investigating on the web alternatives. Before long more considerable plans of action developed; seek marketing1 and online business was the new conceivable outcomes. Upgrades in focusing on Advertising, and seeing how sites look after guests, ended up important. Exploring shopper's conduct and purchasing designs online started to intrigue researchers.

Because of the promotions accessible today, and additionally broadband usage in many homes, promoters can make gigantic jumps and make worldwide crusades.

The actualities are: The Internet is not any more a medium of "new economy", and "E-business" as a term has rather been rendered old. The Internet is utilized as a part of all enterprises, as a marking and marketing apparatus, as an interior specialized instrument, and as the beginning of most business exchanges. Today organizations utilize the Internet as a standout amongst the most capable apparatuses in a major number of ways. The Internet has opened countless alternatives and better approaches for featuring the essential parts of anything. Subsequently marketing has been reclassified through the Internet, and allowed even private ventures to advance and brand their items on a bigger scale. The Internet has in this way experienced tremendous development in online marketing, since its commencement in the mid 1990'ies. It is still however executed in the standard one-route correspondence, as it has dependably been finished.

Examples of overcoming adversity in marketing are anything but difficult to discover: Amazon is utilizing their clients to advertise items to others through "alternate buyers, who looked, moreover looked". Coca Cola are describing by methods for the Internet, MasterCard use silly fastens, and through that viral showcasing.

As a computerized showcasing technique, SEO considers how web seek instruments work, what people examine for, the bona fide ask for terms or catchphrases made into web records and which web look devices are upheld by their focused on get-together of people.

Refreshing a site may consolidate changing its substance, HTML, and related coding to both expansions its hugeness to particular catchphrases and to discharge limits to the requesting activities of web records. Lifting a site to manufacture the amount of back associations, or inbound associations, is another SEO procedure [49].

Web marketing (Internet Marketing) is a general classification of Advertising that may incorporate web index marketing (SEM), site improvement (SEO), email marketing, pennant marketing, web-based social networking. SEM and particularly pay-per-click marketing (PPC) are quickly developing marketing techniques for a wide range of organizations, and it's no big surprise: PPC is generally simple to do in-house, versatile and very cost-proficient—if done accurately.

So what's the "right" approach to do PPC as a feature of your Web marketing procedure? Actualizing a couple of present day marketing best practices will guarantee that your Web marketing endeavors exhibit solid ROI?

- Start with strong catchphrase inquires about: Keyword look into is the establishment of effective Web marketing. Ensure yours is customized and information driven.
- Group and arrange your watchwords: Keyword gathering empowers significantly more vital Web marketing for both PPC and SEO crusades.
- Commit to progressing, iterative Web marketing: To see consistent advantages, ensure you're persistently refreshing and enhancing your pursuit crusades.

A remarkable catchphrase management and inbound marketing system can assume a part in your pursuit marketing methodology.

The study specially aims to determine the significant role of information technology in concern marketing pattern of house hold product. In line with, the objectives of the study are-

1. To determine the extent to which information technology will be contributed to customer satisfaction and house hold product industry.

2. To determine how skillful and knowledgeable the person or staff will use for information technology

3. To decide if there is an expansion in the level of lack and viability of activities since the presentation of data and electronic innovations in house hold item advertising framework.

In the latest decades the PC has transformed into a crucial in moderately every house. We have come to depend upon it in various parts of our life from talking with allies and relatives to perform better in our movement or school. It has advanced toward getting to be bit of our lives so much that enormous quantities of us don't imagine how our lives would be without it. The Internet has transformed into a fundamental consistent everyday presence. Books, reference books and sometimes even newspaper kiosks have been a little bit at a time supplanted by the Internet. They call it 'the information interstate' and we rely upon it to find the answer for our request, to find entrancing information, to share our understanding and in this way advantage from someone else's data, to meet new people (commonly far away). The Internet has made the world a smaller put since now it's less difficult to talk with people starting with one end of the earth then onto the next.

As it can be seen every day the world is advancing. Things are not the same as they were 10 or even 5 years back. This is something you have to notice and endeavor in your business also as you do in your

53

regular day to day existence. The endless usage of the web has made it an unassuming yet to a great degree significant asset for your showcasing targets. Email showcasing, exceptional offers, infrequent advancements, media promoting, all these essentially cost a little measure of what their detached accomplices cost. As a rule you ought to just contribute time. The world is changing, and it's changing further bolstering our good fortune. You basically need to keep a sharp eye and snatch the open entryways as they present. The amount of focuses with respect to Information Technology inside the business it supports is on the rising. Its part is continually progressing and has changed basically from the days when the IT affiliation was consistently insinuated as "data taking care of." Today, in various endeavors, IT engages a couple of associations to isolate themselves from their adversaries.

**Study Procedure:**

To pick the exploration strategy we allude to the proposition made by Galliards identifying with the kind of research to be received in connection to data systems. In his proposition, the creator plots the significance of the utilization of contextual investigations as an exploration system for the examination of hierarchical angles; procedures which might be distinguished as the most widely recognized technique for subjective research used in IT considers. The examination system chose for the accomplishment of the previously mentioned destinations is, regardless, subjective. Specifically, it will be chosen to utilize the contextual investigation strategy adjusted to build up the hypothesis through the comprehension of the wonder in its appropriate setting.

The exploration of this examination is distinct. The information are assembled in various courses: from the resource report and wage proclamation of the organizations; from government workplaces; from a study among the E. Advertising customers, E. promoting planners and the suppliers and the effects of Information innovation in the composition. The expert tallied, scored and sorted out each one of the responses in the gave diagram questions. The examiner drove the investigation really with the respondents. Support library investigate using associations' data, government workplaces, books, journals and magazines was passed on to see whether they reinforce the basic data assembled to show a clearer photograph of the Information innovation's effect on E. promoting.

Numerous parts of Web marketing, however specifically PPC seek marketing and SEO, start with watchword look into the revelation and investigation of words and expressions that individuals utilize while looking for a specific item or management. The watchwords particular to your market or vertical may appear glaringly evident; however you'd be amazed how regularly presence of mind falls flat with regards to catchphrase research and inquiry marketing. Conceptualizing and instinct won't cut it for the genuine Web advertiser you have to go down your choices with true information.

So where do you find that information? Most Web advertisers swing to a modest bunch of catchphrase recommendation apparatuses, similar to Keyword Discovery and the Google Ad Words watchword instrument. In any case, these outsider watchword apparatuses aren't really the most ideal approach to achieve your catchphrase examine. They can really put you off guard for Web marketing, abandoning you with catchphrase information that is:

- **Inaccurate:** These devices restore a restricted rundown of exceptionally summed up, mainstream watchwords that aren't really significant to your business specialty. Also, the movement details are questionable evaluations.

- **Static:** Most catchphrase instruments are worked for one-time utilize couple of clients backpedal and refresh their examination.

- **Non-exclusive:** Finally, any freely accessible catchphrase devices give openly accessible watchword information. Would you extremely like to construct your Web marketing methodology with respect to precisely the same as every other person? Where's the upper hand in that?

There's a superior method to investigate catchphrase open doors for your site marketing: Listen to your guests! You can mine your own site information to get the most precise, pertinent catchphrases for your business. What's more, the best part is, your catchphrase research will be totally restrictive and private, so you can rehearse Web marketing with a sharp aggressive edge.

Word Stream's catchphrase disclosure arrangement parses the private information in your Web investigation and log records to manufacture your watchword database. Since these are the real watchwords that genuine individuals have used to discover your site, you'll know you're constructing your Web marketing choices in light of the correct information.

Successful Web Marketing - Most Web advertisers get a handle on the significance of watchword inquire about, however the significance of catchphrase gathering to pay-per-snap and SEO crusades is seriously undersold. Successful division and association of your watchword scientific classification can have a tremendous effect to your Web marketing comes about. Here's the reason:

- Increased pertinence: It's considerably less demanding to compose particular, pertinent Web duplicate and PPC promotions for small, directed catchphrase gatherings.

- Increased introduction: Ads and points of arrival that are exceptionally pertinent to the pursuit inquiry accomplish higher rankings, more impressions and higher navigate rates (CTRs).

- Lower costs: Search motors compensate exhibited significance and high CTR by additionally supporting your promotions and pages in the SERPs and bringing down your cost per click—so your Web marketing is more practical.

Word Stream look marketing programming is an amazingly productive methods for gathering your catchphrases. Our pursuit marketing devices really propose suitable watchword bunches in light of recurrence and significance (i.e., the measure of movement as well as objectives those catchphrases are driving). You can see these gatherings and make them by clicking a catch; the product naturally sorts handfuls, hundreds or thousands of watchwords as per your particulars and composes your gatherings and subgroups into an envisioned progressive system.

Web marketing is somewhat similar to marriage. You truly do need to continue working at it possibly not for whatever remains of your life, but rather positively for whatever length of time that you need to see picks up in Web activity and Sales. Static catchphrase records and inquiry battles will net you static outcomes, so genuine Web advertisers need to focus on nonstop exertion.

With Word Stream, your watchword research will dependably be a la mode and extending each day with negligible time speculation on your part. How is this conceivable? Simple: You simply introduce a small JavaScript tracker on your site, and Word Stream will consistently track new guests to your site and import them into your watchword database. With a developing, advancing watchword scientific classification, your Web marketing materials from site duplicate to pay-per-click content advertisements and past can advance too.

To get to the impression of house hold item clients in India as for the web marketing managements rendered, a poll overview is directed. The investigation in light of essential information base accumulation yet a portion of the data with respect to web marketing and items will be utilized from auxiliary data sources like diary, books, article and so on.

The terms Computer; Internet; Extranets; Information Technology; Computer Security; Electronic Marketing utilized as a part of research work.

## SAMPLE SIZE

The researcher inquire about work depended on essential information examination and for that researcher is utilized irregular inspecting strategy for metropolitan urban areas of India. The proposed consider was having a place local state and region of researcher. There was 1500 respondents' information gathered to discover the key bits of knowledge.

The present world relies upon the unmistakably to the extent the computerized region.

## SIGNIFICANCE OF THE STUDY

Data innovation has an imperative central purpose to the headway of innovation which has influenced vehemently in fundamentally all aspects of the world economy too in Indian economy also.

With the expanding globalization of retailing, both as far as their purposes of-offer and their purposes of-supply; the Information technology (IT) spend in the retail part has expanded fundamentally. IT assumes an undeniably critical part in the management of complex retail tasks.

Market learning, and additionally control of information and data, is critical to acquiring an upper hand in the retail division. Markets are proceeding to develop and turn out to be more mind boggling; the straightforward procedure of retailing has begun to convey further developed retail data systems to adapt to every one of the exchanges included.

Today, retailers need to change their IT abilities for different reasons, including:

- To increment the organization's capacity to react to the advancing commercial center through upgraded speed and adaptability.
- To gather and break down client information while improving separation.
- To work adequately; retailers require one system working crosswise over stores (or even crosswise over national outskirts) to ensure the best utilization of stock and enhance business forms.

Retailers are starting to see that technology's part is one of an empowering influence. Basically, Information technology can accelerate forms and convey cost sparing advantages to the organization. The retail business faces numerous particular difficulties identified with IT management, including:

➢ **Customer information**

Numerous retailers battle with data over-burden since they're required to gather and filter through mass measures of information, at that point change over it into helpful data in a client driven industry.

> **Transparency and following**

Retailers must expand straightforwardness between systems, and additionally get better following to incorporate systems from producer through to the purchaser while acquiring client and Sales data.

> **Global information synchronization**

Because of radio recurrence ID/electronic item coding, the whole store network has turned out to be cleverer. Retailers must empower the utilization of ongoing information to watch stock levels, Likewise, radio recurrence recognizable proof labelling positions the organization to have the capacity to defend its shipments by enabling items to be followed from producer through the whole production network.

> **PCI Security Compliance**

PCI Security Compliance tends to the retailer's inside security setup and practices, keeping in mind the end goal to moderate payment security dangers. Each business occupied with charge card payment handling is required to conform to PCI Security Standards. On the off chance that a retailer gathers or stores MasterCard data that progresses toward becoming traded off, the retailer may lose the capacity to acknowledge MasterCard payments. Other conceivable outcomes incorporate claims, protection claims, wiped out records, and government fines.

The retailers who exploit outsourcing IT will acquire ideal exhortation and advantages from outsourcing. Numerous retailers have turned towards IT outsourcing as an approach to control costs and enhance their management conveyance.

The eminent use of E-Marketing in India gives a making vision to online customers. This suggestion intends to address fundamental perspectives with respect to the piece of the Internet in essential authority, effect of the Internet on Consumer Behavior, Post Purchase Behavior, the Consumer Decision Making Process and Websites sense of duty regarding the Brand, in light of the way that if E-Marketers need to create in the Online Domain, they should be stressed over the factors impacting the Indian online buyer, their desire to meandering on the web, sorts of lead when they meander on the web and the association between these buyers, by then they also build up their E-Marketing procedures to change over expected customers into dynamic ones.

Those associations that utilization IT for high ground every now and again differ from their opponents in two courses concerning their IT affiliations: they consider IT to be a key business enabling impact as opposed to as a cost center, and they work to help the capability of their IT errands so they can focus their assets on offering some advantage to the business and respond to the current state of rapidly changing business conditions. As to, the piece of Information innovation can't be over supplemented. Over the span of late decades, unpretentious changes in the theory and routine with respect to promoting have been in a general sense reshaping associations. These movements have moreover been evident in advertising and administration related information frameworks. To a regularly expanding degree, associations are looked with the need to control an ever greater and rapidly changing promoting condition. The information taking care of requirements of associations are stretching out as their engaged environment end up being all the more capable and insecure. To manage the extending external and internal information stream and to upgrade its quality; associations should misuse the open entryways offered by show day Information innovation (IT). Data innovation has a key part to play in new versatile affiliation structures, for instance, key associations and cross-commonsense frameworks. While new affiliations will be arranged around business shapes rather than valuable requests, we obviously have a need furthermore for new sorts of IS in showcasing. Honestly, IS will be the establishment of another approach to manage advertising. Henceforth administration and frameworks makers should be better aware of the streets open to consolidate advertising and administration shapes in new creative ways. The inspiration driving this examination is twofold: in any case, it takes a gander at the effects of Information innovation on E. showcasing; next, it tries to demonstrate distinctive possible results to enhance use of IT in E. showcasing.

India is likely watch the splendid time of the Internet section between 2013 to 2018 with incomprehensible advancement openings and normal improvement gathering for E-Commerce, Internet Marketing, Social Media, Search, Online Content, and Services relating to E-Commerce and Internet Marketing. As we in general know, India has far to go in the domain of Digital Marketing as a regularly expanding number of Indians are putting vitality in the web when appeared differently in relation to China and US.

Planned to build up the subjects purchasing conduct, by asking how regularly they purchase on the web. Their intellectual state of mind towards online marketing is likewise included by inquiries concerning consideration regarding marketing and decision to peruse additionally down into an offer. We anticipate that the consideration will be small, however have picked answer alternatives in content, where it is available to elucidation. Our comprehension is that most organizations have not known about the issues with online "on request" state of mind. It is vital to hold the subjects consideration once you have been guided to the Advertising site. For example – an advertisement for a shabby flight, should lead straightforwardly to the booking system, as opposed to another page with additionally marketing for the same (or unique) flight(s). We are not capable, nonetheless, to test this to its maximum capacity, as it would require the plan of a whole site, and to get the details would require a particular knowledge into the organizations' upper hands.

We likewise need to test the sites' capacity to keep their guests, not as in we require guests to remain for long stretches at once, however more to ensure that they don't discover other comparable destinations after their visit. We assess that clients are very faithful towards a site, in the event that it has the alternatives every guest stamp generally imperative. Right off the bat we need the subject to characterize with their own words, and after that we give 10 cases of things destinations can have, and by giving them a chance to pick three of these as most essential, we can test if for example personalization is critical. The whole information is encased in Survey supplement, yet we have here drawn out a couple of remarks from our populace:

This examination postulation centers around concentrate the goals of the customers to wander on the web and their distinctive practices when they peruse on the web. This will help the advertisers and associations to comprehend the different measurements of E-Marketing which help the purchasers in shopping on the web. It demonstrates how the shoppers choose to buy items and features the exercises that happen previously, amid, and after the buy of the item. Associations will profit by creating appropriate systems and picking the correct model to guarantee that customers invest critical energy in the authoritative sites to make the buy.

**HYPOTHESIS**

Marketing is a societal procedure, which perceives buyer's needs, concentrating on an item or management to satisfy those needs, endeavouring to form the customers toward the items or managements advertised. Without a doubt, marketing is crucial to any organizations development. The marketing groups (advertisers) are entrusted to make customer attention to the items or managements through marketing procedures. Unless it gives careful consideration to its items and managements and shoppers' socioeconomics and wants, a business won't more often than not thrive after some time. Basically, marketing is the way toward making or guiding an association to be fruitful in offering an item or management that individuals want, as well as will purchase.

In this way great marketing must have the capacity to make a "recommendation" or set of advantages for the end-client that conveys an incentive through items or managements. All through this investigation we won't vary between marketing, marketing and the term advertisement. Our comprehension of the words is intended to be the same, and subsequently they will as often as possible be utilized. One term should be clarified however; popular marketing, which is an idea that have created with the rise of the Internet. Regardless of whether entertaining, amazing or with profound effect numerous small messages, pictures or even recordings are sent starting with one client then onto the next for different reasons. Viral marketing will be talked about in detail later.

In the marketing division corporate as merchants and makers utilize PCs in their everyday activity to give nature of management to their clients vis the utilization of digital technology. Information technology has likewise enhanced clients learning about the utilization of PC and different devices through which client of house hold item

64

can get to their necessity and make request and payment anyplace on the planet. The business segment enabled and gifted HR can likewise create.

1. The use of information technology has a significant effect on the operation of business.
2. The use of information technology has a significant effect on the operation on household products business.
3. The use of information technology has not significant effect on the operation of business
4. The usage of IT has not a significant role on the operations on household products business.

**LIMITATIONS OF THE STUDY**

All through this examination on the web and disconnected will allude to regardless of whether the subject is accessible to the general population by means of the Internet. We won't consider in what "dialect" (HTML or other) the data is accessible, nor will it be considered, what gadget the data is brought from. The Internet isn't just accessible on PCs. PDAs, mechanical date-books, compact music players and so on are coordinating speedier and quicker.

Online correspondence today isn't just restricted to the PC, thus marketing can be given to the end-client in more routes than by means of the PC. This examination won't recognize distinctive methods for getting to the Internet. A site can be intended to seem best on a smaller screen (PDA), or visit can by means of the Internet go from PC to normal telephone, even with one end writing in content and the opposite end talking. Internet marketing will in this way be utilized as a part of the broadest term conceivable, just where fundamental will the definition be expressed and examined. We have chosen to utilize universally situated Danish organizations in our concern plan. A universally situated organization is characterized as any organization that is as of now working on the worldwide market or is entering the global market, and looks to illuminate the objective clients about its merchandise and enterprises. The explanation behind utilizing Danish organizations is triple, initially it is our local nation, thus the discourse will be less difficult, any requirement for going to or subsequent meet-ups will be easier, also Denmark as a country is a standout amongst the most created on the planet with regards to IT, both foundation (number of broadband clients), open management and the private segment is accessible on the web. Purchasers are expecting on the web arrangements, for banking, basic supplies, data, benefit and so forth. Thirdly we feel that despite the fact that these purchasers are expecting (and getting) online answer for about each part of their life, the procedure of most Danish organizations are not in a state of harmony with what is accessible and asked.

# 4      Analytical Discussion

In the past 50 years, Households have received a few technologies. Some undeniable cases are family machines, for example, washers, dryers, and coolers; amusement arranged items, for example, TV and stereo; transportation and specialized gadgets, for example, vehicles and phones. These technologies have had an assortment of effects on the family. A portion of the technologies have supplanted' difficult work, some of them have essentially lessened it, and a couple of others have changed absolutely the character of the House hold.

In keeping an eye on the critical interdisciplinary written work on House hold advancements we find three interrelated points: the association between family innovation and

1. Time hold stores,
2. Women's business, and
3. Sex-associated division of work.

The first and noteworthy subject relates to the potential that some family propels address in saving time in the execution of housework. Morgan et al. (1966) found families with more modified home mechanical assemblies assessing a bigger number of hours of housework than those with less machines. Robinson et al. (1972) and Vanek (1978) also reported results midway avowing this result. Obviously there are a couple of illuminations for such abnormal revelations. Walker (1969) has suggested that during the time the aftereffect of housework has achieved an unrivaled quality (e.g., cleaner articles of clothing, clean house, kitchen, et cetera.) and to an enormous degree this has been made possible by more up to date advances. Also, there is by all accounts an exchange off of more redundant and routine housework to a more administrative kind of action. Along these lines there is by all accounts a move in inward assignment of the housewife's opportunity.

The other subject that goes through a portion of the examinations needs to do with the connection between current House hold hardware and ladies' work. Strober and Weinberg (1980), battling that utilized spouses use diverse techniques to lessen time weights, tried the speculation that they claim more tough merchandise than non-employed spouses. It was, regardless, discovered that the life partner's business was not basic either in the purchase decision or in the measure of employments on durables. The examination was rehashed by Nichols and Fox (1983) whose revelations attested Strobe and Weinberg's examination.

A third subject relating innovation to family appears in the written work on sex-associated division of work and women's business. Buyer masters have been looking at the division of work and women's business. Customer researchers have been inspecting the division of work at home the extent that a couple enthusiasm for various House hold works out (Davis and Rigaux 1974; Davis 1976; Ferber and Lee 1974; Spiro 1983; Wortzel 1980). The general push of the dispute presented by most makers is that the changing parts of a couple have realized some endeavor centered developments. In this discussion there is little say concerning what part innovation has played in permitting or limiting joint activities. Some social analysts have battled that computerized family innovation has an important effect unfaltering with the upkeep of sex-associated parts in families, meanwhile making

68

it attainable for women to work outside the home (Thrall, 1982; Vanek, 1978). Zimmerman and Horwitz (1983) have resonated a near thought with respect to the creating Information innovation and its impact on the family. "What will women do inside the 'creative house'?

The part advancements play in the bleeding edge House hold. It will in like manner reveal to us the potential that the advances address in altering family stream. For our discussion we think about five estimations:

1. (an) Instrumental versus Expressive;
2. Task Oriented versus Delight Oriented;
3. Passive versus Dynamic;
4. Unifunctional versus Multifunctional; and
5. Low Social Impact versus High Social Impact.

**Instrumental-Expressive:**

The instrumental-expressive estimation is a modification from Parsons' game plan of illustration factors (Parsons, 1951) The instrumental piece of innovation considers it to be a gadget which meets some specific utilitarian destinations of the family. All together that a given innovation may be utilized viably to recognize instrumental targets, one can put that the customer has the learning of how the technology can be used, can adapt to the mechanical requests and really utilizes it to meet particular practical needs. A few cases of instrumental objectives are: require accomplishment, assignment execution, cost funds, and proficient utilization of time. For instance, the phone grants individuals to lead business and build up prompt contact with others at extraordinary separations. Additionally it permits two-way correspondence and accelerates exchanges. Such cases can be accommodated different items too. The instrumental measurement of PCs would allude to their application in an assortment of employments, for example, management of home exercises, word handling, family instruction, and keeping up different budgetary records that serve money related limits.

The expressive side of innovation implies the potential results that innovation makes in passing on sentiments and affections and conveying family related regards through conclusions and in addition lead. People participate in preoccupations and energy as a strategies for passing on their assessments toward others. Such activities have a high individual and mental noteworthiness concerning the House hold.

A hypothesis appropriate to the expressive-instrumental estimation is that Households consider both expressive and instrumental needs in the gathering and use of advances. In any case, the agreement between the necessities changes with each situation. Traditionally, propels which are rich in their capacity to fulfill both expressive and instrumental needs are in all probability going to be more fundamental in a House hold.

Undertaking Oriented-Pleasure Oriented: Technologies can be depicted as task orchestrated or delight arranged, Generally speaking, task arranged advancements are not pleasurable. The nonappearance of satisfaction is gotten from the possibility of the endeavor drew in with using the innovation.

Regardless of the way that there is an association between embraced charm estimation and uninvolved dynamic estimation, they are not the same. Specifically, errand arranged advancements incorporate a movement of manipulative advances and conceivably repetitive exercises. For example, Fried and Molnar (1975) have perceived three interesting components that delineate the task estimation:

1.  Serial trademark variable,

70

2.   Operations-yield relations variable, and

3.   Output outline variable.

The essential variable communicates that continuous direct outline is assessed on a transient scale (i.e., turning the light switch versus divider mulling over). The second factor measures how much exercises that convey yields are depicted by their separation. The last factor insinuates how much the assignments are at risk to reutilization. Thusly the endeavor centered nature of innovation suggests the specific exhibitions the customer needs to perform before the innovation can be put to proposed use. The task presentation of the innovation is also directed by the key motivation for the innovation. For example, most House hold errands are task arranged. Cooking, washing, cleaning are obligatory exercises and the headways that empower these exercises to be performed (e.g., microwave stove, garments washer, vacuum cleaner) may be named task organized because of the possibility of the work. Another instance of undertaking centered innovation incorporates physical work at an enduring rate. Advancements can similarly be task arranged in perspective of the exhaustion factor included.

**Uninvolved Active:** Technologies can be designated detached or dynamic from the customer point of view. All things considered, dormant advancements require less human control and less physical or insightful effort as for the customer when diverged from dynamic innovations. For example, a vacuum cleaner needs human affiliation the distance yet the articles of clothing washer does not. While human intervention is one portion of reserved/dynamic estimation the other fragment relates to the effort required to work a particular innovation. Most House hold advancements require unimportant academic effort in light of the fact that their fundamental limit is to routinize endeavors.

On the other hand they may require differing degrees of physical effort from low to high.

The choosing typical for detached innovations is the limit of the customer to have the ability to be a recipient of the yield of the innovation without having to truly control its creation. Another typical for the standoffish innovation is the probability for the customer to be involved with various activities while up 'til now controlling the mechanical development.

An instance of inert innovation is TV. The effort required by the customer to participate in TV seeing is to some degree unimportant. While the TV is still on, there is no that the watcher needs to do beside kick back and watch it. The vehicle, of course is an instance of dynamic innovation. While the auto is in development, the driver is totally had with its execution and is relentlessly buy controlling the diverse limits. Various diverse advancements in the family have a position some place near the two.

The buyer affirmation of a particular innovation isn't only managed by the latent or dynamic nature of the innovation. There are diverse estimations of the innovation which ought to be considered. Be that as it may, one can create an impression that different things staying measure up to, the buyer would favor a latent technology. Or on the other hand more particularly, given two variants of a similar technology, it is protected to state that the individual would incline toward the detached to the dynamic form.

**Uni-utilitarian Multifunctional:** Technologies can likewise be delegated uni-practical or multifunctional in view of whether they are intended to play out a solitary capacity or various capacities. A capacity alludes to the assigned reason for the item and its useful importance typically decides undertaking suggested by the reason and the item mark as a rule includes its significance. A few items suggest a group of implications we have a solitary significance spoke to by the item, at that point we call the thing unifunctional; else it is multifunctional.

For example, most home machines are uni-functional. Automobiles can be called multifunctional because of the induced gathering of suggestions. In spite of the way that autos are vehicles used for transportation (i.e., single limit), they can be used for work or for voyaging or for shopping, these various activities are perceptually irregular and in addition are pertinently exceptional. Thusly, cars can be called multifunctional. TVs ran moreover be thought about multifunctional in perspective of the adaptability of the programming, for instance, delight, news, preparing, culture, et cetera. Home PCs are doubtlessly multifunctional. There are a couple of unmistakably identifiable specific usages of PCs which make it legitimate to arrange them as multifunctional.

Multifunctional innovations increase the multifaceted idea of undertaking administration for the family. They require more essential manipulative limits and incite a more elevated amount of imaginative dependence. For example, when an auto isolates, there is a more conspicuous crisis in the House hold that when a toaster isolates. Meanwhile, multifunctional advancements incite a more conspicuous wellspring of satisfaction because of the amount of assignments they can perform.

Social Impact: Some headway has had more conspicuous social impact than others. Social impact insinuates the manner by which existing techniques forever are changed. The more noticeable the impact, the more essential the change, All advances make an impact or some resemblance thereof. For example, the TV innovation has influenced the media penchants for the all-inclusive community, recipient perspectives and direct toward delight and the association between relatives. Home devices appear to have had a lesser impact however the auto had an essential impact. We talk about the vehicle culture as if a whole extent of characteristics and lifestyle outlines have made around the auto. The level of social impact caused by an innovation implies that the significant built up nature of the innovation. New advances may endeavor to make new life plans, change o]i life illustrations or ensure the present life outlines. To the extent that they attempt to change old life outlines, they meet with remarkable assurance.

To gather, the standard stresses of House hold innovation have given cautious thought to time administration and save reserves and the impact on women's parts in the House hold. We assume that while the association between family innovation and time administration is essential, there are diverse components that need examination since they choose to an imperative degree the determination, use, and impact of innovation. To begin with, there are family progresses which are not undertaking centered and where time estimation may not be as essential. Second, exhibit day families are constrained to be more sure and live in a more atomistic condition than groups of earlier conditions. This infers within structure of the House hold ought to be broke down exactly. Third, the basic duty regarding machines, which has been the examination point of convergence of a bit of the buyer investigators, adds alongside no to the understanding of House hold/innovation relationship. The factor that ought to be assessed is the level of usage and the reasons behind such use.

The regular approach of audit family/innovation relationship is obliged e, the nature of allotment of advances. We assume that in order to develop a noteworthy examination of this relationship one must go past irrelevant gathering and take a gander at the entire methodology including appointment and the cases of use and also the impact of innovation on House hold movement. In this examination, we attempt to conceptualize this issue by proposing a model of House hold innovation structure. Introduced in this structure is the House hold social space. The examination takes a gander at the associations between the three sections as an approach to understanding the family/innovation relationship.

There has been a growing excitement for late years among purchaser examiners in family lead and usage. A particular piece of the family usage which is the essential point of convergence of this examination is the use of innovation in the House hold. A maj or purpose behind think the House hold innovation relationship has been obviously communicated by Nicosia (1983): "Innovation is typically associated with creation shapes and distinctive human science disciplines have explored the effects of innovation in work activities.... The effects of innovation in use practices have been, all things considered, neglected or taken for granted.... By focusing on the family as the institutional setting for a considerable measure of client lead, we should get a prevalent cognizance of the interdependencies among innovation and consumers...."

A surge of eagerness for innovation and Households has been initiated by an arrangement of factors. The area of married women into the work drive has made the probability that families may get a more critical number of proficient contraptions. Sometime-spending research has moreover been represented in Europe and in the U.S. looking issues. The ascent of present day Information innovation, for instance, videotex and home PCs has mixed much unmistakable interest and what's more coherent interest.

These processes rely on three premises. In any case, in understanding the House hold innovation relationship, the standard approach has been to look at the House hold and not just the innovation. A balanced approach would require that we take a gander at the possibility of the House hold and also the qualities of family propels.

Second, we have looked for after a line of thinking in our examination which tries to perceive the three methods: choice, use, and impact of innovation concerning a littler scale social framework which is known as the House hold. While determination is a fundamental portion of the innovation/purchaser interface, it gives however a lacking photograph of the totality of the interface itself, just in light of the fact that it is compelled to the hidden periods of customer contact with the innovation. It is this stress the entire system merits examination.

Third, we set that Households have internal ecologies and regard frameworks which turn out to be conceivably the most critical factor in accepting new advances. In spite of the way that a changing of exogenous (i.e., outside to the family) and endogenous (i.e., internal) powers isn't extraordinary to the family, the particular manner by which it is refined isolates families from other social foundations.

In the accompanying region we discuss a couple of issues from current written work. This will be trailed by a presentation of a model of the family creative structure and a change of the relevant considerations.

This prompted the making of Consumer Traits and Online Shopping Issues Model. These model endeavors to mull over the Issues of Online Shopping which mirror the varying Consumer Traits of the customers. The customer profiling was done on the information collected utilizing K-Means Cluster Analysis with the assistance of Weighting Technique. Social occasions were cleared: Apprehensive Conservatives, Flamboyant Conservatives, Internet Savvy Risk Averse and Internet Moderates.

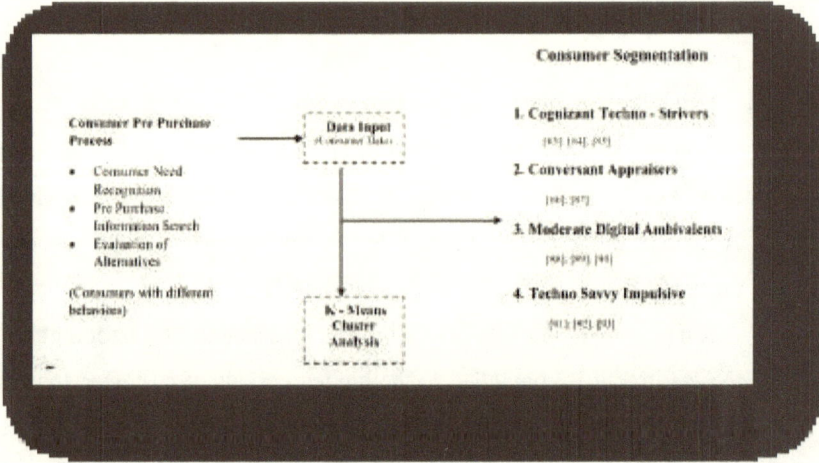

Fig 2: Consumer Segmentation (CTOIM) [58]

**Emanant Model of E-Marketing and the Consumer Decision Making Process** The Website Attribute Index (WAI), Website Brand Contribution Model (WBCM), Consumer Prepurchase Model (I-CPPM) and Consumer Traits and Online Issues Model (CTOLM) together incorporated every one of the discoveries of the exploration and build up an Emergent Model (Fig 3). This will help the organizations to understand the behavior of the consumers and the relation between marketers and consumers. The Fig 3 represents that the Consumer is at the centre of the emergent Model and there exists a bi-directional relationship between the consumer and the four dimensions of the Model. These four dimensions are the individual models developed during the research study and are now playing the

77

role as the important pillars of the final emergent model. It shows that if the consumers are more internet savvy, they will be influenced by the Website Brand Contribution dimension, where attributes and website parameters play an important role in influencing them.

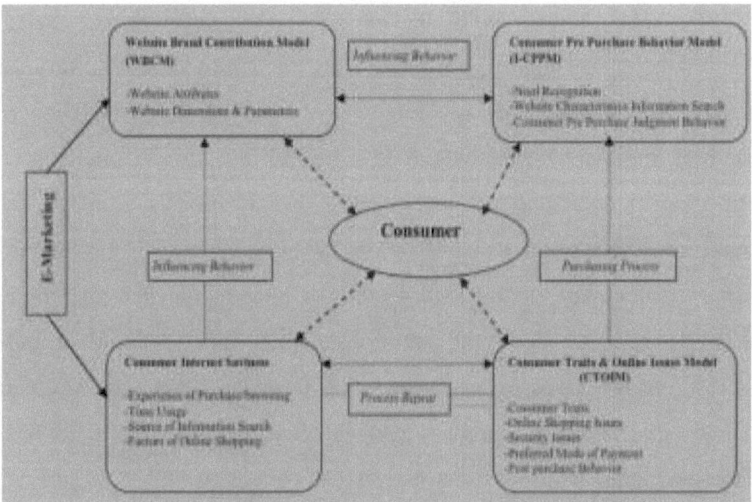

Fig 3: Emergent Model of E-Marketing and the Consumer Decision Making Process

On the off chance that buyers are happy with the site characteristics and parameters, they will be impacted towards the Pre Purchase Process, where they will perceive their necessities in the wake of going to sites and will discover wellsprings of data pursuit and approaches to assess their data to locate the best alternative for buy and afterward move towards the buy choice where they manage the shopping issues and attributes, select the best method of payment and take the choice to purchase the item/benefit from the went to site. They exhibit their post buy conduct and on the off chance that they are happy with their buy, they have positive conduct towards the site and the other way around and their buy procedure closes here. In the event that they need to rehash the procedure, this procedure will proceed similarly.

78

This model endeavors to demonstrate how Consumer Behavior and E-marketing are connected with each other. This rising model was certainly enabling the associations to know the vital periods of the buy to process.

The House hold technologies can be installed in a multidimensional space. Various family technologies along various measurements talked about before. We accept such an introduction is helpful in situating technologies in a typical multidimensional space. Keeping in mind the end goal to make examinations reasonable we have utilized a solitary classification "home apparatuses" for washer, dryer, dishwasher, cooler, and so on., in light of the fact that these items appear to be found rather indistinguishably along various measurements. To assess practically an assortment of promotions as per some understood examples and position them along a few measurements which permit correlations paying small heed to the particular idea of the technology,

Likewise, we can assess promotions as far as their appropriation potential as well as far as their real utilize. The idea of assessing advances or items on various properties isn't new. Key to most purchaser investigate is the idea that customers settle on item appropriation choices in view of item qualities. In this way a car is acquired utilizing some standard criteria, for example, miles per gallon, seating limit, styling and so on., however such ascribes are one of a kind to a solitary item, vehicles. Be that as it may, when we start to look at House hold promotions, such item particular characteristics don't bode well. We, along these lines, need to digest the credits of promotions to the basic level of exercises which are implanted in the totality of the House hold system.

A few endeavors have been made in the past to group family durables into total classes. Market analysts have customarily examined House hold durables as far as necessities and extravagances. "Necessities are characterized as those products which are purchased in similar amounts paying small respect to changes in costs or livelihoods" (Douglas and Isherwood 1979), the refinement is to some degree simulated and specialized and maybe excessively shortsighted. For instance, an extravagance today can without much of a stretch turn into a need tomorrow. Additionally, an extravagance for some might be a need for others. Additionally, what is embraced as an extravagance may end up being a need after proceeded with utilizes while in the meantime a need may turn into an extravagance in some uncommon cases?

We are more in concurrence with the qualification proposed by Hendrix (1984) between "time purchasing" and "efficient" promotions. An impediment of this order for our motivation, in any case, is that such a measure is restricted to promotions where time management is basic. This isn't valid for all the House hold advances.

## RESEARCH FINDING AND ANALYSIS

This section was mainly focusing on the demographic characteristics of the study area in terms of sex of the respondent, caste, income, education age.

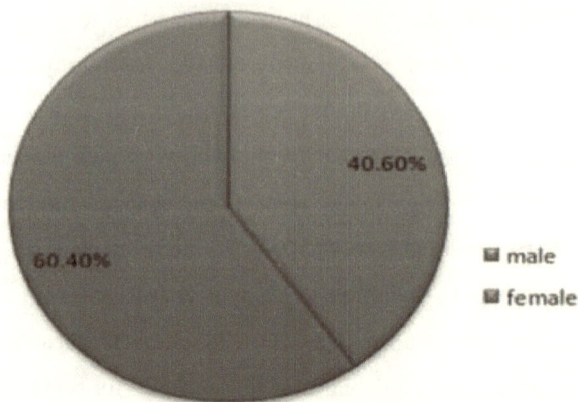

**Figure 4: Sex ratio of the respondent**

       1500 respondents were mulled over for the investigation. The diagram portrayal demonstrates the level of male and female who are doing on the web and disconnected shopping. It demonstrates 40.60% of male go for the shopping while 60.40% female do the shopping. This implies a greater amount of the female part required on the shopping. This gives a general thought of the sex proportion who is more associated with shopping.

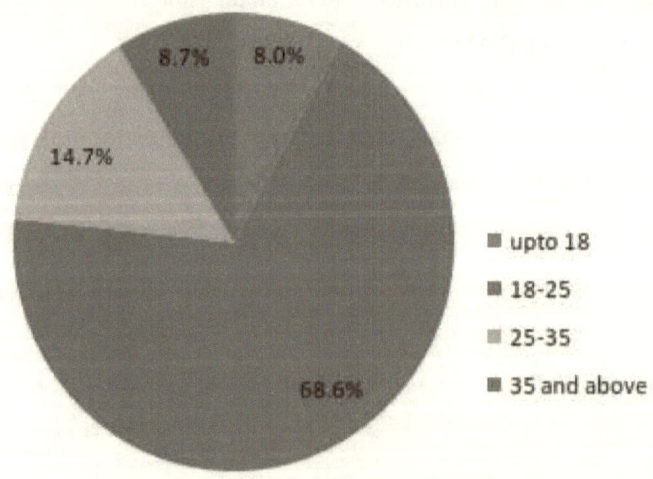

**Figure 5: Age of the respondent**

The above graphical portrayal demonstrates the age classification of populace who pick internet shopping .The major of clients who utilize online shopping to satisfy their need goes for the most part between 18 to 25 age classification including 68.6% of the aggregate customers and this is for the most part observed among them in view of the expanding mechanical insurgency among the adolescent populace and they can utilize this technology for their prosperity more than other age gather class. Next the age gathering of 25-35 contributes as the second most shoppers compose utilizing internet shopping managements of 14.7%. For this age gather time is the central point for utilizing them this stream as approach to shop. Whatever remains of the buyers are age gathering of 35 above and 18 beneath involving 8.7% and 8.0% individually. The level of populace low in light of the fact that the greater part of the 35 above gathering have absence of sufficient learning of technology utilized. What's more, for 18 underneath cash requirement comes into picture.

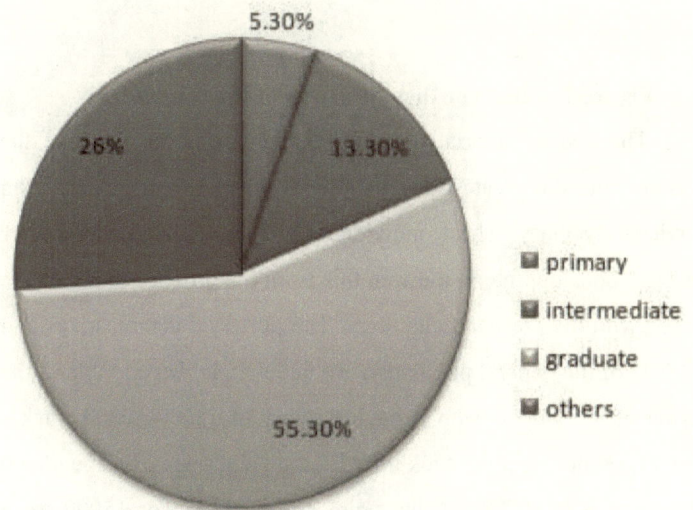

**Figure 6: Qualification of the respondent**

The above pictorial portrayal demonstrates the capability of the respondent, and the most extreme capability is others that is graduate individuals which comprise around 55.30%.next is the others which is around 26% they are of Ph.D. Masters and so on. The middle gathering which comprise of 13.30% and the essential gathering comprise of 5.30%.Qualification is a central point for online shopping, unless and until the point that the individual is sufficiently qualified to get to the web. They can't do internet shopping

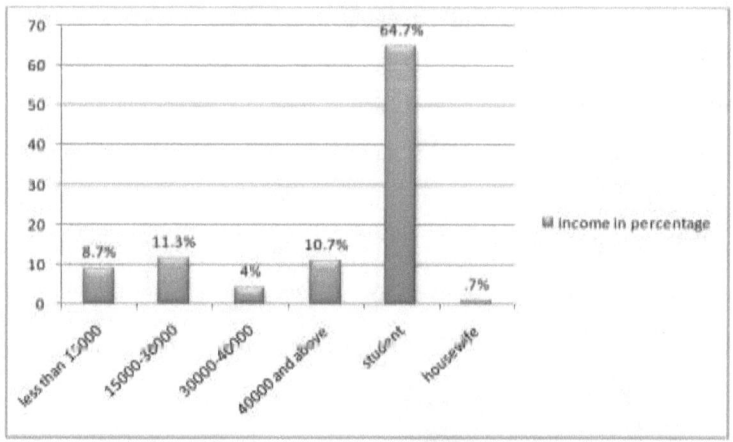

**Figure 7: Different Income group of the respondent**

The above pictorial portrayal demonstrates the wage of the respondent, and the greatest pay for the shopping site originates from the understudy class. These individuals are not utilized rather they ponder and do shopping on the web this is on the grounds that they are refreshed with the present technology. The portrayal demonstrates that the 64.7 % of the general population are understudy. Second comes the gathering of individuals who is having salary of 15000-30000 it takes around 11.3% at that point took after by the gatherings of wage 40000 or more which is 10.7%, at that point comes the under 15000 wage bunch which secured 8.7%,and after that 30000-40000 pay gathering and last comes the housewives which takes 4% and 0.7% separately. Housewives don't go for the online shopping as they don't get time out of their House hold work and they are additionally not mechanically refreshed. The chart gives the obvious thought regarding which salary amass is more into the online shopping.

**Table 1: Reason for doing online shopping according to the age group**

| Age of the respondent | Time saving | Door to door service | No issue of going to shop | Availability of product | Total no. of respondent |
|---|---|---|---|---|---|
| Up to 18 years | 20 | 40 | 30 | 30 | 120 |
| 18-25 years | 290 | 230 | 190 | 320 | 1030 |
| 25-35 years | 60 | 30 | 50 | 80 | 220 |
| 35 and above | 30 | 30 | 20 | 50 | 130 |

The overview led on 1500 clients of various age aggregate about the components that draws in them to incline toward online shopping. Out of 120 clients up to age 18 years old, 20 said its efficient, 40 gave the reason as way to entryway management, and 30 said they don't have to go outside to the shop for the buy of merchandise and 3 think items are effectively accessible on the web.

**Reason for doing online shopping according to the age group**

- Time saving 8%
- Door to door service 17%
- Total no. of respondent 50%
- No issue of going to shop 12%
- Availability of product 13%

The 1030 client maturing in the vicinity of 18 and 25, 290 said its efficient, 230 gave the reason as way to entryway benefit, and 190 said they don't have to go outside to the shop for the buy of merchandise and 320 think items are effectively accessible on the web. The 220 client maturing in the vicinity of 250 and 350, 60 said its efficient, 30 gave the reason as way to entryway management, and 50 said they don't have to go outside to the shop for the buy of merchandise and 8 think items are effectively accessible on the web. The 130 client maturing over 350, 30 said its efficient, 30 gave the reason as way to entryway benefit, 20 said they don't have to go outside to the shop for the buy of merchandise and 50 imagine that the items which they are getting is effectively accessible at on the web.

**Table 2: item that never purchased from online web sites**

| Age of the respondent | Clothes | Electronic items | Books | Footwear | Total no. of the respondent |
|---|---|---|---|---|---|
| Up to 18 years | 10 | 70 | 30 | 10 | 120 |

| 18-25 years | 190 | 370 | 330 | 140 | 1030 |
| 25-35 years | 80 | 60 | 60 | 20 | 220 |
| 35 and above | 50 | 60 | 20 | 0 | 130 |

Out of 120 customers up to age 18 years of age, 10 said its Clothes, 70 said Electronic items, 30 said books and 10 said its footwear.

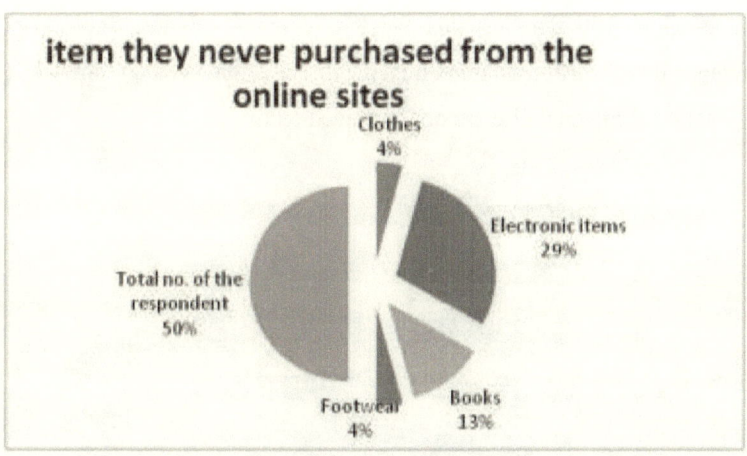

The 1030 client maturing in the vicinity of 180 and 250, 190 said its Clothes, 370 said Electronic things, 330 said books and 140 said its footwear. The 220 client maturing in the vicinity of 25 and 35, 80 said its Clothes, 60 said Electronic things, 60 said books and 20 said its footwear. The 130 client maturing over 35, 50 said its Clothes, 60 said Electronic things, 20 said books and none said its footwear.

**Table 3: Preference of the respondent for the shopping sites according to the delivery of the time**

| Shopping sites | Yes | No | Total |
|---|---|---|---|
| Flipkart | 610 | 120 | 730 |
| Snap deal | 320 | 40 | 360 |

| | | | |
|---|---|---|---|
| Amazon | 220 | 10 | 230 |
| Myntra | 90 | 40 | 130 |
| Jabong | 30 | 00 | 30 |
| Others | 20 | 00 | 20 |

On asking Customers which online business site they like to buy stuffs and do they convey products on time730 clients said they shop from Flipkart with 610 saying that merchandise are conveyed on time while 120 denying this fact.360 clients said they shop from Snapdeal with 320 saying that merchandise are conveyed on time while 40 said that merchandise are not conveyed on time.

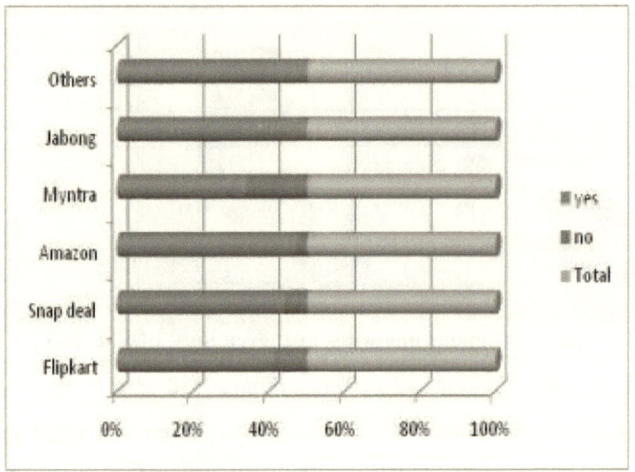

230 clients said they shop from Amazon with 22 saying that products are conveyed on time while just 10 said that merchandise are not conveyed on time. Out of 130 individuals shopping from Myntra 90 said yes merchandise are conveyed on time and 40 said no. All the 30 clients who shop from Jabong said that merchandise are conveyed on time. While 20 clients shopped from different sites and are happy with the correct conveyance on time.

**Table 4: online shopping sites according to the delivery of time**

| Shopping site | 5-8 days | 8-10 days | 10-12 days | More than 12 days | Total |
|---|---|---|---|---|---|
| Flipkart | 240 | 330 | 100 | 60 | 730 |
| Snapdeal | 160 | 100 | 70 | 30 | 360 |
| Amazon | 100 | 90 | 40 | 0 | 230 |
| Myntra | 70 | 30 | 20 | 10 | 130 |
| Jabong | 10 | 20 | 0 | 0 | 30 |
| others | 10 | 0 | 10 | 0 | 20 |

On asking Customers "What is the base day of passing on a thing to you?" Out of 730 customers who shopped from Flipkart, 240 said it took Flipkart 5-8 days to pass on their stock, 330 said it is between 8 to 10 days, 100 it took 10 to 12 days and 60 said it assumed control 12 days.

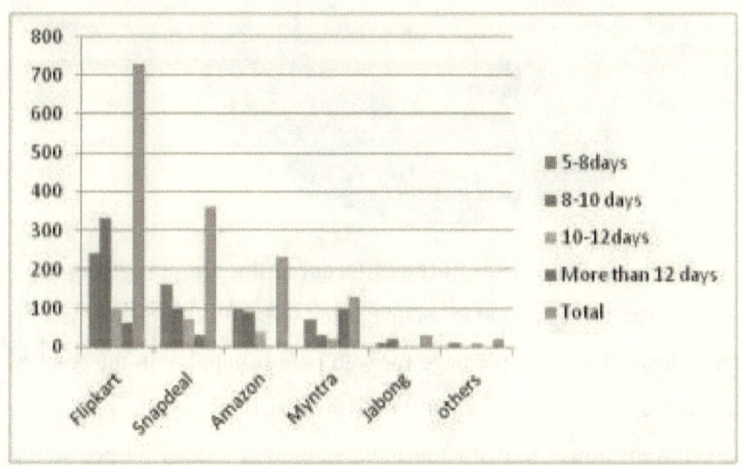

Out of 360 customers who shopped from Snapdeal, 160 said it took Snapdeal 5-8 days to pass on their items, 100 said it is between 8 to 10 days, 70 it took 10 to 12 days and 30 said it assumed control 12 days. Out of 230 customers who shopped from Amazon, 100 said it took Amazon 5-8 days to pass on their stock, 90 said it is between 8 to

10 days, 40 it took 10 to 12 days and no customer said it assumed control 12 days. Out of 130 people who shopped from Myntra, 70 said it took Myntra 5-8 days to pass on their stock, 30 said it is between 8 to 10 days, 20 it took 10 to 12 days and 10 customer said it assumed control 12 days. Out of 30 customers who shop from Jabong, 10 said it took 5-8 days to pass on their items, 20 said its between 8 to 10 days, No one said it assumed control 8 days. While 20 customers shopped from various destinations, 10 reported items were passed on in 5-8 days and other said it assumed control 12 days.

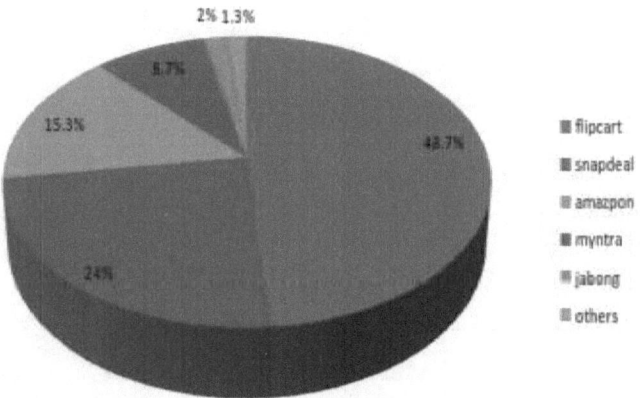

**Figure 8: Preference of the different online shopping sites**

The most supported webpage for web based shopping is Flip kart as it was the principle page for web based shopping in the country for quite a while later when distinctive districts came into picture its market went down, still it's the most supported site as its promoting done suitably with overwhelming brand nature of things and administrations over various goals .So, it's up 'til now prepared to hold the market. The accompanying comes the snap deal site where around 24% of customers lean toward it. This is an immediate aftereffect of the current extending promoting technique of the site and a certification to give better administration and thing. Next comes amazon site which secured 15.3% of the all inclusive community, it is an online shop mammoth outside the country still its attempting hard to publicize its picture in the country, and ensures a critical potential for grandstand in not all that far off future. Next online areas favored are myntra and jabong and the level of the all inclusive community are 8.7%% and 2% independently. it has come into picture of web shopping because of its support offers and favorable circumstances it gives. Negligible number of rates is 1.3% for other shopping areas like – Yepme, craftvilla.com and distinctive goals.

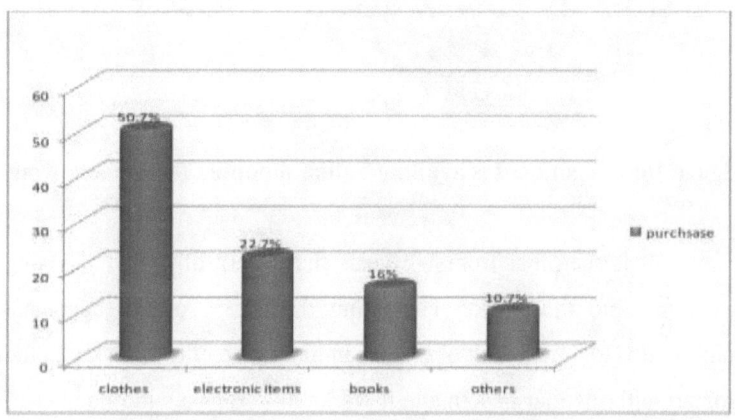

**Figure 9: Mostly purchased goods from online sites**

The customers for the most part buy garments online containing 50.7% of the populace, The expanding interest of garments online is a result of the assortment of alternatives the buyers get the opportunity to pick and that to at a sensible cost. Besides the quality gave is likewise prevalent. Thus, there is an interest for garments in online pages .Next comes the electronic things buy with 22.7% of the aggregate request. These destinations give these things at processing plant yield cost and furthermore give a guarantee over the things .So, purchasers think that its sensible to get it on the web. The following interest happens to books containing 16% of the request. Alternate items bought online spreads for 10.7% of the aggregate things acquired online like – footwear, beauty care products, and so forth.

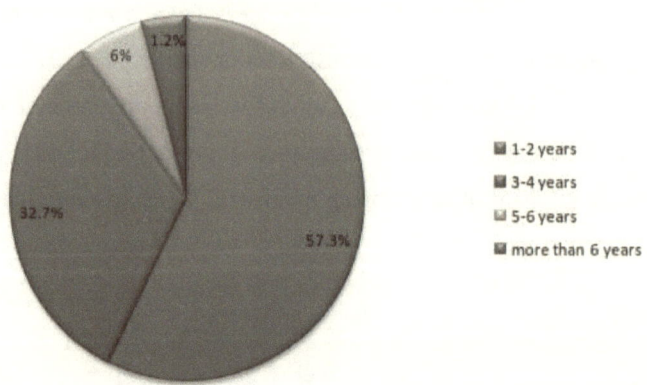

**Figure 10: Respondent is availing online shopping for the following year**

It is seen that from 1-2 years the pattern of online shopping has come into the market containing the 57.3% of the aggregate number. It is a direct result of the expanding range of technology to the ordinary citizens that have made it workable for expanding number of populace choosing on the web buy which was not seen before in 5-6 years when it was seen just 6% went for online buy of items . In past 3-4 years when technology was raising it was seen that about 32.7% changed to online marketing of items. Furthermore, in 6 years when technology was controlled by few it was seen that lone 1.2% of aggregate did internet shopping.

Late examination demonstrates that because of expanding need of society and time requirement has driven the greater part of the populace change to internet shopping. It is seen that almost 44.7 % of the normal populace do purchase the item in each 2-3 months at a

91

general interim. 34.7% of populace do online shopping each month which is a direct result of the accessibility of wage and technology to do shopping. Additionally, 10% of populace do online shopping each week and 4.5% once in a year.

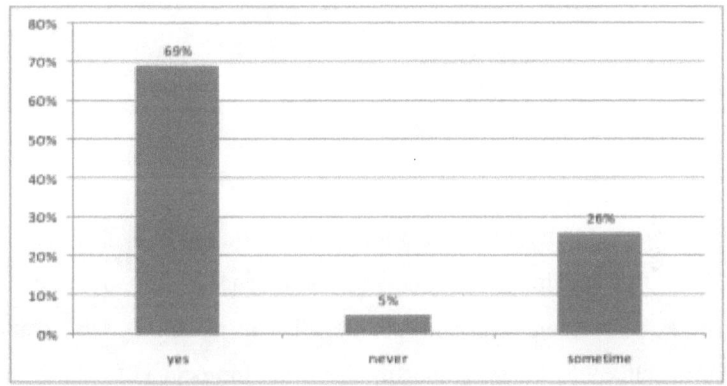

**Figure 11: Is website providing the sufficient information?**

Each item which is accessible for buy on a specific site gives all around educated data about it alongside pictures to pull in the clients about it. The greater part of the circumstances the site give each significant data required and commonly its maintained a strategic distance from when the item isn't up to the stamp in 69% of the cases it was seen that each data required is given which makes the item directed easy to use and a client can purchase the item wisely. Just in 5% cases it was seen that the item data isn't given and 26 % of the respondent said that it give the data at some point.

**Marketing on the web**

The greater part of the distinctive methods for Advertising are recalled, a few could specify particular brands or sort of items being promoted. Be that as it may, relatively few respondents could recollect talk/gathering Advertising.

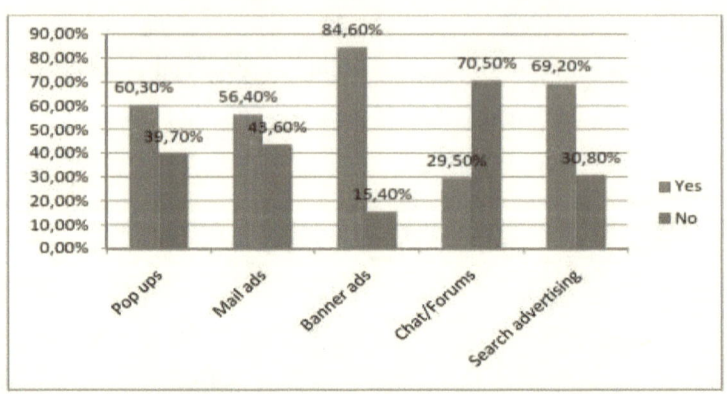

**Figure 12: Perception of marketing online**

We see this as an issue with the absence of promotion, more than it isn't recognized and additionally other online Advertising choices. It could be intriguing to see the information of "standard" media, for example, TV or news study's. Commonly, sites are seen a larger number of times than that of a marketing segment between appears on TV, or on a particular page in the news study. In any case, these media reuse their commercials every day, even hourly (most pertinent to TV). Hunt Advertising is the thing that we find in Google, Yahoo et cetera. Pennant advertisements and inquiry Advertising, this sort of pursuit marketing is recollected by the most the reacted.

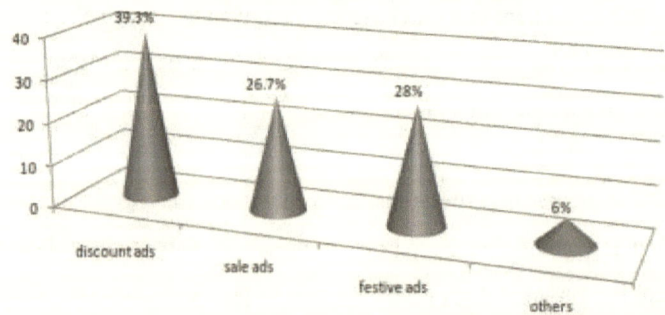

**Figure 13: Type of advertisement mostly attracts to purchase online**

93

Notice assumes a noteworthy part to make a site a brand in the market. Besides, promotion pulls in its client towards them to make salary. The sort of publicize that draws in the client towards them is rebate promotions which is 39.3%, which give the client motivation to purchase their items at sensible costs. Additionally the business advertisements bring more clients almost 26.7% of aggregate client gets pulled in to it. The bubbly season is the time span amid which major of the populace do their shopping is 28% and if promotions identified with it is distributed then it conveys more client to them.

**Preference of the respondent for the shopping medium**

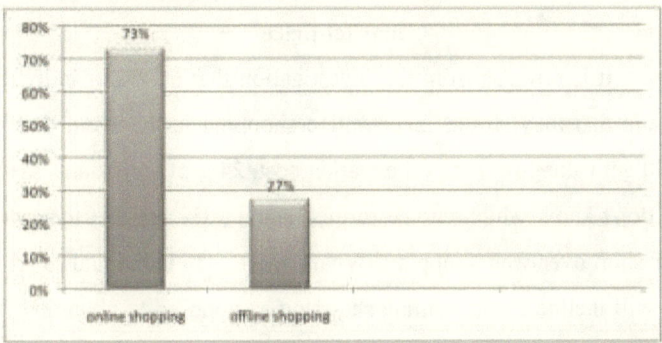

**Figure 14: Preference of the respondent for the shopping medium**

From the above graph it is clear that out of 1500 respondent 73% respondent need to go for web based shopping as they think that its more advantageous and simpler for them yet 27% client need to experience the disconnected shopping since they are more agreeable in conventional market.

94

**Preference of online shopping when price lower than market price**

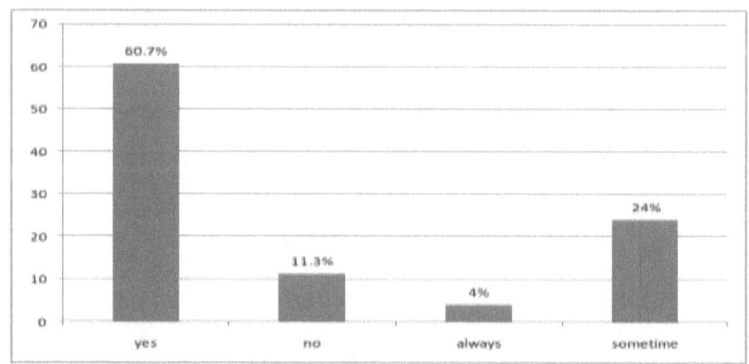

**Figure 15: Preference of online shopping when price lower than market price**

It is obvious from the investigation that 60.7% of individuals concede that they would favor online shopping in the event that they would get value lower than the market cost. 24% of individuals say that they don't know which choice to pick and 11.3% say that they would favor shop over web shopping. What's more, 4% individuals said that they will incline toward online shopping as opposed to obtaining from disconnected shopping or conventional market.

**Does online shopping is as secure as traditional shopping?**

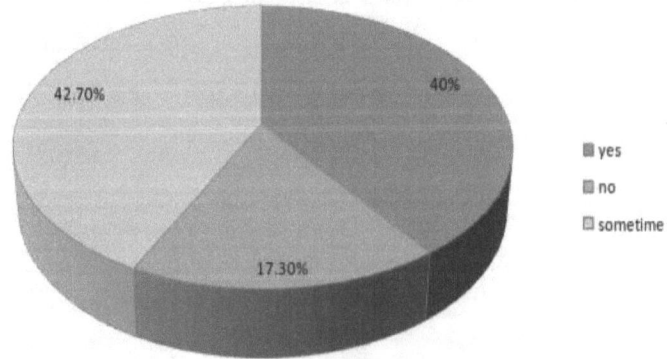

**Figure 16: Does online shopping is as secure as traditional shopping?**

95

The Graph obviously demonstrates what clients think about online shopping, with 42.70% at some point think it's safe at some point it isn't when contrasted with conventional shopping.40% client think online shopping is as secure as customary shopping, while 17.30 % trust it isn't secure.

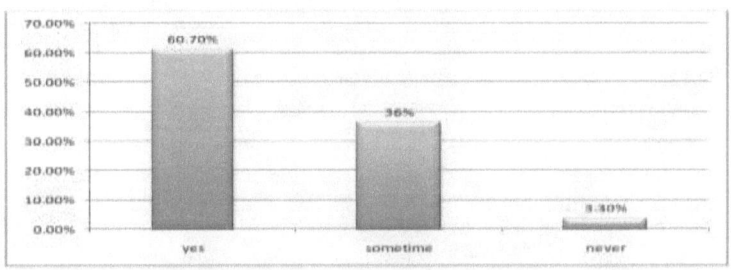

**Figure 17: goods on internet as compared traditional market**

60.70% clients trust that online shopping you get more assortment of merchandise when contrasted with customary shopping, which thus is less tedious as you can investigate numerous things/products in only a tick , while 36% clients imagine that the online shopping doesn't generally give you assortment of things to buy , they still to some degree have confidence in conventional shopping. Despite the fact that online shopping has its own advantages, yet inaccessibility of web association makes the clients go to conventional shopping. 3.30 % clients never surmise that online shopping gives you progressively or better assortment of item; despite everything they do customary shopping to get the item.

## Type of advertisement mostly attracts shop offline

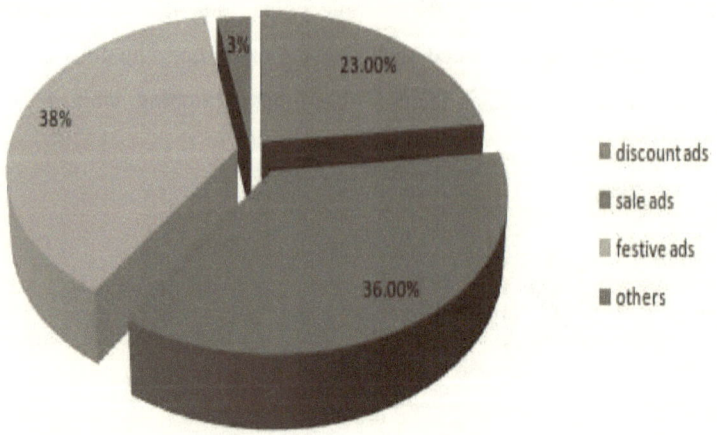

**Figure 18: Type of advertisement mostly attracts shop offline**

There are different reasons why individuals are pulled in to shop disconnected most conspicuous reasons are rebates advertisements, Sales promotions, merry promotions and different varlous advertisements draws in clients to shop disconnected. India where celebrations are viewed as most promising minutes, advertisements assume imperative part in advancing disconnected shopping. happy promotions assumes the real part with 38% in drawing in the clients to go for disconnected shopping, trailed by Sales advertisements with 36% this sort of advertisements are extraordinary occasions to pull in clients by indicating promotions to clients about Sales for a constrained timeframe. The rebate advertisements which conceals 23 % comes alongside Sales promotions in drawing in client for disconnected shopping, While remaining 3% are different various advertisements, for example, off season and so on. Likewise to some degree draws in individuals.

## Chart: Accessing shopping websites

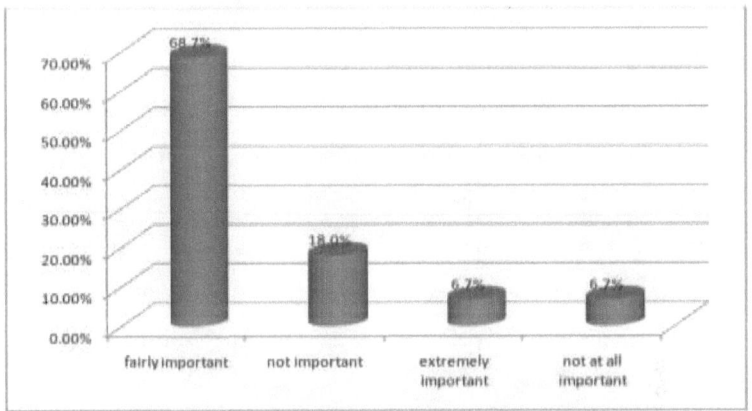

**Figure 19: Accessing shopping websites**

Getting to shopping sites is likewise a parameter deciding the distinction between internet shopping and conventional shopping. While north of 68% individuals believe it's genuinely imperative to get to the shopping sites, 18% believe it isn't so much that essential to get to shopping sites on the off chance that you need to buy anything, they can even buy merchandise by conventional shopping, while 6.7% believe it's vital to get to shopping sites to buy anything, strikingly same level of individuals believe it's not in the slightest degree vital to get to online business destinations.

To guarantee the strength of the ICT coefficients we tried whether the outcomes would hold while controlling for urbanization proportion as opposed to utilizing GDP per capita development.31 Urbanization proportion would influence the quantity of employments accessible, as urban zones tends to offer more openings for work than country territories, and in addition positively affecting the utilization of ICTs, because of practical working of foundation. Also, I am trying a control for power utilization, which is an essential for utilizing digital apparatuses. This control is excluded in the principle relapses because of the constrained measure of perceptions. The outcomes for the two controls are still fundamentally strong for mobiles and web, yet the coefficients are diminishing some with power. Counting power notwithstanding alternate controls, power turns not out to be noteworthy. In conclusion, we tried the legitimacy of my outcomes supplanting the training control, normal years of tutoring, with the proportion female to male enrolment in essential and auxiliary instruction and aggregate enrolment in tertiary instruction. In spite of much lower measure of perceptions, the outcomes still hold for web, yet not for cell phones.

Confirmation from my information recommends that ICTs in creating nations did not begin spreading impressively until the start of 2000. The World Bank has assessed that the quantity of web clients tripled from 2005-2017, and it may be a probability that restricting the day and age to these years will change the outcomes, particularly to develop nations. Analyzing the web first; when testing for the two distinctive eras I get intriguing outcomes that bring up new issues for future research. On the total level web's impact on the female to male interest proportion is certain and noteworthy the first day and age 1991-2005 yet not critical from 2005-2014. Disaggregating the impacts for money statuses web had an around square with minimal impact for all pay bunches from 1991-2005, expanding the proportion by 0.05 rate point for a one-unit increment in web clients. From 2005-2014, low-salary nations encountered a huge abatement in the proportion of female to male work drive support from a one-unit increment in web clients. The minimal impact in high pay nations did not change much from the first day and age.

These outcomes propose that the digital separation between nations has been developing from 2005 and onwards, where created nations appear to have embraced to profit by the chances of ICT, while creating nations are lingering behind. Running comparable tests for cell phones, they had a beneficial outcome for the female to male proportion for most nations from 1991-2005, with most astounding impact in high pay nations. For 2005-2014 the total, worldwide effect of mobiles diminishes the sex proportion by 0.01 rate focuses. This is clarified by negative, critical impact for cell phones in low and low center wage nations, and no impact for more created nations. Likewise, mobiles do never again appear to enhance sexual orientation uniformity in the work market, and appeared to be most imperative in the early years of ICTs.

ICTs appear to be a positive commitment in expanding sexual orientation equity in the work showcase at the worldwide, total level. ICTs, expanding in greatness from cell phones to web, increment the proportion of females to guys. The enhanced sexual orientation balance is predominantly because of an expansion in female work compel cooperation, yet web had the extra impact of diminishing male interest at the worldwide level. These outcomes are in accordance with past writing, which is rational in the constructive outcome of ICTs on work constrain investment, particularly for expanded female support, reviewing a portion of the investigations in view of House hold studies, they all discovered generous upgrades and open doors for females to take an interest in the economy, both in created and creating nations. The discoveries sum up the outcomes, and make them tantamount crosswise over nations; however the impacts are significantly lower than discoveries from most exact examinations. Results from my relapses demonstrate that ICTs affect is fairly low; just expanding the female to male proportion by 0.04 rate focuses for web and 0.018 for cell phones. Despite the fact that these outcomes probably are at the lower limits of the real impacts, because of the descending predisposition, they are still low. It is absolutely difficult to measure what is a 'high impact' and what a normal effect of ICT ought to be. All things considered, contrasting the impact of ICTs and the coefficients of instruction from similar relapses, an extra year of training appear to have substantially higher effect for sex correspondence in the work advertise than a one-unit increment in ICTs. Other monetary and social speculations, for example, training, may as needs be more useful for sexual orientation uniformity than ICT. Despite the fact that my discoveries can sum up comes about crosswise over nations, they do in all likelihood experience the ill effects of inner legitimacy, implying that the estimator of the causal impact may be one-sided and conflicting. It is a worry that expanded female work constrain investment, and enhanced sexual orientation uniformity, might be caused by other puzzling components than ICTs. We can't finish up causality in this proposition, however the course of causality is upheld by discoveries from past examinations and is agreeable to my speculation, Internet, contributes decidedly to sexual orientation uniformity in all statuses at the total level, while mobiles have a more unobtrusive impact. The most intriguing bring about analyzing the statuses of business is that ICT does not appear to have any impact on female possess account specialists, regularly thought about business people. Despite the fact that the sexual orientation proportion is expanding with web, this isn't as per an expansion in female business visionaries, yet rather a lessening in guys. A portion of the examples of overcoming adversity from the writing and the worldwide advancement banter about are that ICTs conceivably can make open doors for ladies as business people, beginning up organizations, expanding their benefits, and offering their items at online markets. Exact, econometric investigations have been uncertain in ICTs impact on independent work. My outcomes be that as it may, don't discover an expansion in female possess account specialists. Further, it could be contended this may be something to be thankful for in regards to ladies strengthening. Claim account specialists in high-pay nations are considered business visionaries and representatives, frequently respected high-status. In poorer nations, ladies ventures are regularly observed as a transitory pay until the point that a more ordinary work opportunity is accessible (Duflo and Benerjee, 2011, p.226). Given that female claim account specialists are not expanding; this may infer that they have found better openings for work for instance in formal business.

The impacts of ICTs are expanding with level of advancement, and digital technologies have no impact for sexual orientation balance in low-wage nations.

In low-salary nations, the expansion in the female to male proportion is caused by abatement in male investment, not by initiating more females to work. These outcomes are conveying important bits of knowledge to the global advancement face off regarding, and intriguing approach suggestions. This proposes ICT may not be the impetus engaging ladies in creating nations arrangement producers was seeking after. It appears that a nation must have a specific level of advancement, keeping in mind the end goal to exploit ICTs open doors for engaging ladies. There are a few conceivable clarifications why the impact is bringing down in creating nations than created. Data and correspondence technologies initially progressed from created nations, where the technology could be viewed as an endogenous change; an aftereffect of the monetary procedure itself. For creating nations, the quick spread of ICT then again, can be viewed as an exogenous impact in a nation, produced outside their monetary procedure. It is in this manner a plausibility that the general advantages from overflows in advances shifts. Plausibility for the distinction in impacts could be absence of foundation ventures. This clarification would likewise be in accordance with late discoveries from the Asian Development Bank (2017, p. xix), that economies needs extraordinary sort of foundation as they create. Low-salary nations would put resources into water, power and sanitation speculations before putting resources into ICTs. As indicated by my information, web entrance in low-wage nations has expanded from 0.6% all things considered in 2000 to 21.4% of every 2017 and from 4.7% to 53.9% in low center salary nations. This recommends it more likely than not been a few interests in foundation the most recent fifteen years, however perhaps insufficient to take full preferred standpoint of it, or possibly just amassed in for instance the huge urban areas. As a rule, it appears like creating nations have not outfitted in their capacities to adequately bridle their technology speculations. This would clarify why the negligible impacts from ICTs were roughly equivalent before 2005, yet built up a colossal separation in affect the years 2005-2014. This subsequently addresses ICTs as a potential jumping system for creating nations. Despite the fact that ICTs speaks to easy routes for correspondence and data potential outcomes, this does not naturally reflect in different parts of life, for example, working life. Fruitful alternate routes are uncommon and not really ready to generously change the work advertises in creating nations. ICTs may not, or if nothing else not yet, be the distinct advantage and impetus it was wanted to be for ladies in creating nations.

**Purchaser power:** Consumer sway is the assertion that buyer preferring decides the maker of merchandise and enterprises. It is the flexibility to decision the item to buy. It is the item which is wanted by the shopper. The request of the item will prompt make of merchandise and ventures. The request will naturally prompt creation. Electronic shopping/Internet shopping/online shopping: Purchasing of products or managements over the Internet utilizing web program, by methods for either a PC or an Internet TV or a mobile phone. It is the acquiring of item through web.

**Purchaser conduct**: Consumer conduct is the investigation of how, when, why and where individuals do or don't purchase items. It tangles components from attitude, human science, social human sciences and financial aspects. It tries to perceive the purchaser decision making process, both separately and in gatherings. It is the decision of the shopper or purchasers to purchase or not to purchase the items.

**Online business:** It comprises of the purchasing and exchanging of items or managements over electronic systems, for example, the Internet and other PC systems.

**Unpracticed customers:** The general population who have in no way, shape or form directed an online buy, as "non-customers". The client who have just experienced disconnected market for buying the items, who have never rehearsed the internet shopping,

**Experienced customers:** The "customers" to individuals who do have acquired from an online webpage, the buyer who have bought any item from any online destinations

**Expectation:** "It speaks to motivational constituents of conduct, that is, the level of cognizant reason that a man will apply keeping in mind the end goal to finish conduct". This is the assurance to purchasing or not to buy the products from on the web or disconnected market.

**State of mind:** "Disposition implies the heading of conduct which reflects as a person's certain or antagonistic valuation of a pertinent conduct and is gathering of a person's critical convictions concerning the genuine significances of performing conduct".

**Impact:** The ability to have an aftereffect of the item or products to the buyer itself. The item or the destinations of internet shopping have that ability to impact the buyer to buy items from on the web or disconnected market.

Entrepreneurs and senior association pioneers comprehend the need to build mark mindfulness, connect with clients, set up thought authority, and produce income (Sales or gathering pledges dollars). Accomplishing these marketing objectives is an immense test, and will probably require some refined marketing activities.

A strong marketing system combined with the correct mix of marketing promotions will enable you to interface with your clients in the best ways and accomplish your marketing and larger authoritative objectives. Digital technologies have irrefutably changed the marketing scene with the capacity to affect your main concern like never before. In any case, there are additionally more instruments than any other time in recent memory... all in all, where to begin?

Here are nine fundamental segments that any association – whether non-benefit, B2B, or B2C – should incorporate with their marketing technology stack. (Not comfortable with the expression "stack"? It just means the entire arrangement of technology and programming).

**MARKETING TECHNOLOGY**

There are a scope of various marketing advances, including those that oversee and track digital marketing endeavors (like Google Analytics), instruments that track and oversee client connections (like

Pipe drive), and program based programming that can help track and oversee online networking endeavors (like Hoot suite).

In the substance marketing circle alone, there are content marketing technology apparatuses for content duration, content circulation, content enhancement, content estimation, and that's only the tip of the iceberg. The same is valid for online networking marketing technology instruments. The sheer volume of apparatuses in the marketing technology space, combined with the hundreds – once in a while thousands of merchants in a solitary class can influence marketing technology to appear to be very scary to those not acquainted with the space.

Marketing technology arrangements for the most part fit into one of at least twelve classifications. Be that as it may, it's normal for present day, complex marketing technology instruments to offer abilities spreading over a few concentration territories.

- Monitoring and examination apparatuses
- Marketing computerization apparatuses
- Customer relationship management (CRM) instruments
- Tag management instruments
- Data management stages (DMP)
- Content conveyance systems (CDN)
- Conversion streamlining devices
- Campaign management devices
- Email marketing stages
- Mobile streamlining devices
- Marketing systems
- Remarketing arrangements
- Search motor marketing apparatuses

Obviously, even this rundown isn't comprehensive. Different sources distinguish other marketing technology classifications, for example, online networking marketing apparatuses, online courses and web conferencing instruments, plan devices and undertaking management devices, cooperation devices, content management systems (CMS), and the sky is the limit from there. Most importantly if there's a marketing procedure, you can wager there's a marketing technology instrument that intends to streamline that procedure. How these a huge number of apparatuses are sorted and characterized is as differed as the instruments themselves.

**Marketing technology apparatuses:**

The most widely recognized sense strategy to finding the correct marketing technology is to first decide the marketing office's needs and afterward obtaining a product stage to address those issues. Group estimate, venture following needs, future business development, and spending plan are immensely imperative components to consider when looking for the correct marketing technology device.

Obviously, viably utilizing marketing technology requires a comprehension of how the purchaser is advancing and which channels is encountering development and why. What methodologies is your marketing group at present utilizing to achieve prospects? What are your KPIs (Key Performance Indicators) and how are they being estimated? What marketing forms are expending the most time? In the event that those marketing forms are delivering ROI, consider marketing technology instruments that automate or streamline those procedures.

In the event that your marketing office oversees heap undertakings and battles at the same time yet does not have a solid strategy for figuring out which marketing systems are best, your first marketing technology venture ought to be in an apparatus that breaks down crusade execution, empowering you to decide how to apportion your marketing spend and which marketing technology devices can best help your most productive endeavors. Once these experiences are caught, they can help control an association's basic leadership process in picking the correct marketing technologies.

**Procedures and targets with marketing technology:**

Numerous marketing technology arrangements offer a scope of capacities inside a solitary stage, so it's critical for ventures to assess their marketing methodologies and decide how a marketing technology arrangement would streamline marketing endeavors and bolster general marketing and business goals.

Some marketing promotions empower advertisers to lead research and guide battles as indicated by purchaser personas and the different touch focuses all through the purchaser's excursion, computerizing procedures, for example, email marketing with activated messages in view of prospect conduct. Others offer inherent CRM (Customer Relationship Management) abilities or incorporate with existing outsider stages a venture may as of now be utilizing to oversee prospects and clients, taking into consideration a more durable marketing technology foundation for current endeavours that depend on a huge number of devices to take care of business.

Taking off new technology over a marketing group can be a strategic test for associations, so while choosing marketing technology arrangements, undertakings must consider how new arrangements will incorporate with existing instruments and work processes. Adapting new systems and procedures is tedious. At the point when weighed against onboarding prerequisites, the best marketing technology arrangements offer both time and cost investment funds by streamlining existing marketing procedures and lessening the time advertisers spend on different marketing errands.

**Practices in marketing technology:**

It's essential that an organization have the proper structures and capacities to help their marketing technologies. This includes ensuring colleagues have sufficient preparing on the best way to best utilize the technology accessible to them, having the important spending plan for technology acquisition, and notwithstanding employing a committed marketing technology officer to oversee programming devices and help conquer any hindrance between the marketing and IT offices.

A few devices offer various or a suite of across the board answers for help meet an marketing office's some needs. So it merits considering putting resources into a solitary arrangement with numerous abilities that is additionally perfect with your business, as opposed to a choice of shifted stages that could possibly incorporate with each other consistently, if by any means. Adopting this strategy is reasonable and can enable your business to keep away from tedious migraines coming about because of programming contradiction and at last spare cash over the long haul.

**Analytics**

Unless you can gauge the outcomes, don't do it. How and where are you catching, putting away, and assessing subjective and quantitative information about your marketing endeavors? Would you be able to present a business defense to your CFO for why you should keep contributing cash or time? Utilize promptly accessible examination devices, a significant number of which are free, to help manufacture this business case and make your marketing more grounded.

**Mobile**

Portable marketing includes achieving clients on their PDAs and other cell phones through content informing and applications. Organizations can utilize instant messages to send exceptional coupons or arrangements to individuals on a marketing list. While a few organizations build up their own particular marked applications for cell phones, numerous piggyback on existing applications that offer space for promotions or coupons designed for neighborhood clients. For instance, a business may keep up a profile on an online networking cell phone application that gives clients a 20 percent markdown in the event that they experiment with another item at the store.

**Marketing Automation**

An abundance of new programming stages and advances has been acquainted with this space in the course of recent years, requiring impressive marketing ability to completely use. These devices enable advertisers to achieve customers through different channels while mechanizing a significant number of the more redundant undertakings related with executing marketing efforts.

**Content Management System (CMS)**

Your CMS is the place you refresh your site, regardless of whether with pictures or content. This is a zone where you should keep things straightforward and utilize one of the basic stages since they are anything but difficult to utilize, coordinate pleasantly with other marketing programming, and point of confinement your reliance on outsiders to make essential updates.

**Customer Relationship Management Database (CRM)**

This is a minimal effort authoritative device that gives you a chance to be more vital with critical upside. Making fundamental gatherings of individuals in your database will give you a chance to speak with them fittingly. In case you're holding up to manufacture a bigger group before actualizing this instrument, don't! Get your procedures set up now and consider your development while choosing a device by guaranteeing you can send out and move your information later.

**Email**

Email marketing can be a breeze in the event that you set up your email stage to work as an inseparable unit with your CRM instrument. You will abstain from investing extra energy sectioning clients or refreshing contact data when you are prepared to send something new to your contacts, liberating you to center around the email outline and duplicate.

Email marketing is a standout amongst the most moderate and conceivably captivating approaches to advertise an item. Organizations that have developed pick in email records have a substantial base of clients already identity inspired by the items they offer. Email marketing is a perfect method to declare new offerings, convey coupons or rebates and offer data on items. Numerous email marketing efforts have digital into digital bulletins, in which item marketing coordinates with convincing substance.

**Search Engine Optimization/Search Engine Marketing (SEO/SEM)**

Website improvement and web index marketing aren't just about how to get discovered on the web. Today, SEO/SEM specialists enable organizations to upgrade the greater part of their online marketing channels to boost substance and results.

An extensive variety of SEO apparatuses are accessible that give understanding into the online action of your clients and your opposition. We trust it's essential to streamline catchphrases over all channels to convey an effective SEO/SEM procedure usage. In case you're simply beginning, center around catchphrase inquire about and checking the fundamental SEO components of your (site page meta-labels, alt-message on pictures, and peruse benevolent duplicate). Further developed SEO work ordinarily requests contracting a specialist for help.

**Social Media**

As capable as web-based social networking can be, unless you have somebody devoted to dealing with your social nearness, it can be a genuine deplete on your chance. With the normal lifetime of a tweet averaging only 19 minutes, it can appear like a simple movement to drop. Yet, let be honest, a Twitter account that hasn't sent another tweet in three months accomplishes more damage than great.

Online networking is both a noteworthy opportunity and an awesome test for organizations with regards to item marketing. It can be a fast and simple approach to impart data on new items to a vast gathering, yet organizations must be mindful so as to draw in clients as opposed to patronize them. Organizations should take a gander at online networking as technology that empowers the well-established marketing strategy of verbal. Make a convincing web-based social networking knowledge, cooperate with clients and urge them to impart your item data to others.

**In Store**

Technology is making its quality known in stores. The utilization of digital signage is a pattern that enables organizations to catch the consideration of clients and market particular items to them. This is especially useful for eateries and different organizations that need to react to changes in stock or present new items all the time. Propelled purpose of offer systems can give representatives ongoing data on what items are in stock or enable them to track a client's inclinations. Giving fantastic client benefit is a key to fruitful Sales and marketing.

Sites have moved toward becoming business necessities with regards to marketing items. The medium takes into account a lot of space to share item points of interest, audits, photographs and recordings that connect with potential clients. Declarations frequently go out through online managements and media stories, while blog entries and informal exchange can direct people to a site. Organizations can declare items, as well as can offer them specifically to clients everywhere throughout the world. That span extends a long ways past what a nearby daily paper promotion can accomplish.

# 5 Summary and Conclusion

The study uncovers that the male are less doing the online shopping than female. The female are more into online shopping since they appreciate doing shopping whether it is conventional shopping or e-shopping. The mechanical structure of the House hold is unpredictable. It decides

1. The House holds duty and use of time, vitality, and resources to meet its creation and utilization needs,

2. The task of the arrangement of its exercises, and

3. The examples of House hold connections in respect to its generation and utilization objectives.

The model is additionally in view of the acknowledgment that House hold choices to embrace promotions and create proper use designs are impacted by the need to spare time, to oversee proficient tasks, and to render the family as independent as could reasonably be expected. Given that most Households, at any rate in the contemporary western world, are enriched with current family gadgetry, what separates the families from each other is the character of their innovative structure of which the obtaining or ownership of promotions is yet one small segment. As delineation, it appears glaringly evident that as families experience distinctive life cycle designs, diverse technologies become possibly the most important factor. Youthful, single individuals purchase greater amusement arranged technologies; guardians with kids have a more prominent requirement for clothes washers, substantial coolers; et cetera. In any case, such clarifications touch just a small piece of the House hold technology picture. They say next to no in regards to why diverse families with comparative attributes have distinctive utilization designs and distinctive utilization designs and distinctive utilize arrangements of technology. Unless one takes an aggregate perspective of technology in the House hold and looks at how it is implanted in the social setting of the family, the investigation will stay not as much as satisfactory.

The youthful age is all the more frequently obtaining from online destinations as a result of the unrest in the technology among the adolescent populace and they can utilize this technology for their prosperity more than other age assembles class. Flipkart is the shopping site which is more ideal by the youth. There are expanding interests of online shopping in light of the fact that the assortment of choices for the customers to pick and that to at a sensible cost and at some point even less cost than the market. Electronic things were less requested from the e-shopping yet garments are considerably more requested by the buyers. There are a few items which are not conveyed by the shopping destinations in the ideal zone, it is seen that with the headway of the technology the inclination of the online shopping increments. Prior individuals more utilize the customary shopping. Presently additionally individuals who don't know about the few shopping destinations and not that in fact progressed are less into web for shopping.

A valuable conceptualization of a family is that it is where some movement or different goes on ceaselessly when individuals from the House hold are available. Distinctive technologies allow the execution of these exercises at various levels of proficiency and with various outcomes. Up to this point Households were seen as utilization systems. A later way to deal with the investigation of Households has been to view them as both utilization and creation systems (Becker, 1976). The part of House hold technology as a facilitator of the creation and utilization forms is naturally self-evident. It is straightforwardly attached to the different exercises that are a piece of creation and utilization inside the family. A case of an action which is a piece of the creation procedure is feast planning and a related utilization movement is eating. Most family technologies might be seen as adding to the creation procedure in the family. There are additionally advances which are specifically utilized as a part of utilization exercises, for example, tuning in to radio or sitting in front of the TV, and so on.

In spite of the fact that Households were at that point furnished with a large portion of the cutting edge gadgetry by the mid-fifties or mid-sixties, the approach of late data advances have opened up new examples of generation and utilization.

Keeping in mind the end goal to catch the staggering nearness of technology in the House hold we have built a vast example of exercises performed in a typical House hold in a created society and the comparing profile of advances related with exercises. Following Hendrix et al. (1979), we have recognized three sorts of House hold exercises: Inelastic (IE), Intermediate (IM), and Discretionary (D).

The most families are mechanically extremely needy. That is, the occurrence of House hold advances is sensibly high in the normal family. Second, most House hold advances are designed for the generation procedure instead of the utilization procedure. The ramifications of these two discoveries are a few.

The primary concern is, different things being equivalent, that it is so hard to bring new advances into Households particularly when the current level of innovative frequency is somewhat high. If we somehow happened to envision a House hold with a limited mechanical space, each time an technology is added the space keeps on topping off. The nearer the space is to immersion; the more troublesome it is to include advances. Under what conditions is it then conceivable to present new technologies? We theorize that either the promotions ought to have significant differential favorable position or the House holds need to experience basic movements to allow presentation of new technologies. Be that as it may, the circumstance isn't so straightforward. For instance, despite the fact that not naturally self-evident, one can additionally express that the level of occurrence of a House hold technology does not demonstrate a comparing level of utilization. Thusly, new promotions are simpler to present if the level of utilization is high. Households which are dynamic in the utilization of technologies are the ones prone to be responsive to new advances.

A last ramification is that technologies which are more arranged toward generation process in the family are more promptly received and utilized than advances which are utilization situated. The thinking behind this is generation technologies can straightforwardly add to execution efficiencies, for example, undertaking diminishment, time investment funds, decrease in manual exertion, and so forth. Second, more exercises in the House hold are creation arranged than utilization situated. Creation is likewise a more detailed process than utilization. Likewise, rationally, there is by all accounts a nature of excellence related with creation; generation some way or another speaks to esteem included while utilization brings down it. It is effortlessly overlooked, in any case, that in a family the creation and utilization go as an inseparable unit.

The appropriation and utilization of advances in the Household is a component of the qualities (and requirements) of the family and the idea of the technology itself. Customarily, purchaser analysts have concentrated on the selection procedures to the prohibition of utilization forms. The constraint of appropriation models is that they are single even choice models and say almost no in regards to the example of connection amongst Households and technology. Keeping in mind the end goal to comprehend this communication we propose to analyze first the idea of the technology itself and line it up with an study of the family as a social system with its one of a kind Characteristics.

The point of this proposition was to bring some greater lucidity if ICTs affect sex fairness in the work showcase. The outcomes from leading a board information study of 156 nations from 1991-2014, bring helpful commitments for future research and critical approach ramifications of ICTs affect sexual orientation characters. As a matter of first importance, my outcomes infer that an expansion in the offer of ICT clients have a positive effect in narrowing the sexual orientation hole of females to guys taking an interest in the work constrain. In spite of the fact that the impact is low, the expansion in the sexual orientation proportion is chiefly because of an increment in female investment, and frequently moreover determined by a diminishing in guys. As anyone might expect, the web has a higher peripheral impact because of its transformative effect for new open doors for data, decreasing time imperatives and giving new employments. Cell phones have when all is said in done been more compelling in created nations, most likely because of digital mobile phones, yet this are yet to be examined. Cell phones when all is said in done have been of less effect on sex equity the most recent years. While recognizing the impacts by nation pay, I get the most fascinating outcomes. Digital instruments assume a higher part for sex uniformity and female work drive investment in effectively created nations. This is probably in light of the fact that females in created nations with their foundation, abilities and economy can take full favorable position of the open doors from ICTs. For low-wage nations, cell phones have no impact, and the minimal impact for web is low, roughly 1/3 of the impact in high-wage nations. Is it in this way right to presume that ICTs for improvement and ladies' strengthening is a fizzled procedure? A conceivable issue with this study, is that with the accessible information I am not ready to represent the sex digital gap. This isn't really an issue in high salary nations, where the digital isolate is non-existing, however may be of generous effect for nations where females have significantly bring down access to the web than guys, regularly in low-wage nations. I am very much aware this could prompt descending predisposition, and that my outcomes in all likelihood are at the lower bound. The outcomes would maybe be extraordinary if the ICT-information were disaggregated by sex. Nations have begun detailing sex-disaggregated information on ICT utilize the most recent couple of years, and I trust future research on this theme might have the capacity to give a more exact estimation of relationship of female access to female strengthening. Another essential ramifications is that the chances of ICTs for females in creating nations might be in a too soon stage to be caught by these relapses. Recognizing that technology in numerous nations can be viewed as an exogenous stun to an endogenous work market may propose that overflow impacts to female work investment sets aside more opportunity to see the outcomes from than considered in this theory. Ultimately, an imperative issue that ought to be specified is that it won't not be sufficient to think about the support proportion keeping in mind the end goal to say anything in regards to the totality of the ICTs affect for ladies' strengthening with respect to work.

Studies have discovered that offering ladies employments in for instance the new management segment expands the investment rate, however these occupations have a tendency to be low-pursued and unsecure. Concentrate the unpredictability of sexual orientation equity concerning interest, as well as nature of employments and wages may be a conceivable expansion for additionally inquire about. ICTs have with no uncertainty contributed in changing individuals' private and expert lives, both for females and guys. It has prompted more effective markets, bring down exchange costs and less demanding access to data. To completely exploit the open doors ICTs may have for sex balance, my outcomes propose that it is vital with a specific level of advancement, including fundamental system, instruction and wellbeing. A vital strategy suggestion from this is nations must supplement technology ventures with monetary and social changes to get the most extreme advantages from digital advances and in the end a more sexual orientation rise to work advertise.

This study propelled a perfect that utilizations shopper esteem observations to build our mindful of channel decision. Prior work confirmed the key impact of apparent esteem has on buy goals, yet just focused on item or store esteem bits of knowledge. This investigation expands the studys while making the inquiries from the buyer who are into internet shopping and in addition customary shopping to rate both the diverts in the terms of execution, items, time of conveyance, quality and other related parts of on the web and disconnected shopping. By tolerating this approach, agents and specialists can increase profitable bits of knowledge into the inspirations to embrace an unmistakable channel for shopping. A bunch of all client correspondence with items, managements or people that is particular. Another worry was that the reasonable model, a hypothetical setting for the investigation of the hypothetical premise of all the exploration on it is set. Client conduct is a procedure of dialogs with financial specialists to purchase customer merchandise and purchaser conduct proposals of the procedure.

These are the 4 factor of customer support is characterized as:

1.      Person's Features,

2.      Standard of living,

3.      Basic requirements and

4.      Status that specifically motivate the requirements.

The respondents in the present investigation are PC client and heavier Internet clients; they are refreshed of the technology. Online correspondence today isn't just kept to the PC, thus marketing can be given to the end-client in more courses than by means of the PC. This study was recognized diverse methods for getting to the Internet. A site can be intended to seem best on a smallr screen (PDA), or talk can by means of the Internet go from PC to normal telephone, even with one end composing in content and the opposite end talking. Online marketing will in this way be utilized as a part of the broadest term conceivable, just where important was the definition be expressed and talked about.

# 6

# References

1.  Jessica Keyes; Managing IT Performance to Create Business Value; CRC Press Year 2016

2.  Ashfaque Ahmed; Software Study Management: A Process-Driven Approach; CRC Press Year 2016

3.  Kaylene C. Williams; Robert A. Page; Marketing to the Generations; Journal of Behavioral Studies in Business; Year 2017

4.  Knut Holt; Market Oriented Product Technology: A Key to Survival in the Third Millennium,Springer Science & Business Media, -2013

5.  Dr. MahabirNarwal Dr. GeetaSachdeva; Impact of Information Technology (IT) on Consumer Purchase Behavior; Researchers World -Journal of Arts, Science & Commerce; Vol. No: IV Issue: 3Year: 2013

6.  Walter Brenner, Lutz Kolbe; The Information Superhighway and Private Households: Case Studies of Business Impacts; Springer Science & Business Media, 2012.

7.  Michael Baker; The Marketing Book; Routledge, 04-May-2012.

8.  OluwagbemiOluwatolani; Abah Joshua and; Achimugu Philip, The Impact of Information Technology in Nigeria's Banking Industry; Journal of Computer Science and Engineering; Vol. No: 7 Issue: 2 Year: 2011

9.  Vincent K. Omachonu; Norman G. Einspruch; Technology in Healthcare Delivery Systems: A Conceptual Framework; The

Technology Journal: The Public Sector Technology Journal; Vol. No: 15 Issue: 1 Year: 2010

10. Jessica Keyes; Marketing IT Products and Services; CRC Press, Year 2009

11. Venkatesh; Marketing of Information Technology: Concepts, Products, Services and Intellectual Property Rights; Tata McGraw-Hill Education, 2009

12. Ashfaque Ahmed; Software Testing as a Service, CRC Press, 2009

13. Karakaya F., T.E. Charlton., "Electronic Commerce: Current and Future Practices", Managerial Finance, Vol. 27 (7), pp. 42-53, 2001.

14. Mohammed R., "Internet Marketing", McGraw Hill, New York, Vol. 4, 2001

15. Lawson M., "Berners-Lee on the read/write web", 2009.

16. Pingdom R., "Internet 2009 in numbers", April. 2010.

17. Brown J., Hickey K., Pozen V., "An educators' guide to credibility and Web evaluation", 2002.

18. Song J. H., Zinkhan G. M., "Determinants of perceived web site interactivity", Journal of Marketing, Vol. 72 (2), pp. 99-113, 2008.

19. Levin A. M., Levin I. P., Health C. E., "Product category dependent consumer preferences for online and offline shopping features and their influence on multichannel retail alliances", Journal of Electronic Commerce Research, Vol. 4 (3), pp. 85-93, 2003.

20. Bartel-Sheehan K., Doherty C., "Reweaving the web: Integrating print and online communication", Journal of Interactive Marketing, Vol. 15, pp. 47-51, 2001.

21. Srisuwan P., Barnes S. J., "Predicting online channel use for an online and print magazine: A case study", Internet Research, Vol. 18 (3), pp. 266-285, 2008.

22. Martin J. A., "Working offline with Google Docs", 2009.

23. Ricker T., "The Google switch: An iPhone killer", Retrieved November 19, 2009, from www. engadget.com/2007/,01/18/the-google-switch-an-iphone-killer. [12]. Schiffman G. L., Kanuk L. L., "Consumer Behavior", 11th Edition, New Delhi: PrenticeHall of India, Pvt., Ltd. 2009.

24. Solomon M., Bamossy G., Askegaard S., Hogg M.K., "Consumer Behavior – A European Perspective", 3rd Edition, England: Pearson Education Limited, 2006.

25. Blackwell R. D., Miniard P. W., Engel J. F., "Consumer Behavior", Thomson SouthWestern, 2006.

26. Wilkie., "Consumer Behaviour", 3rd Edition, John Wiley and Sons, 1994.

27. Howard J. A., Sheth J. N., "The theory of buyer behavior", John Wiley and Sons, New York, 1969.

28. Mowen J.C., M Minor., "Consumer Behavior", 5th Edition, New York: Prentice Hall, 2000.

29. Mckinsey., "The consumer Decision Journey", Mckinsey and Company, 2009. Synopsis-23

30. Simon H. A., "The New Science of Management Decision", New York: Harper & Row, 1960.

31. Nicosia F. M., "Consumer Decision Processes: Marketing and Advertising Implications", Prentice Hall, pp. 65-75, 1966.

32. Keeney R. L., "Decision Analysis: an overview", Operations Research, pp. 803-838, 1982.

33. Regan P. J., Holtzman S., "R&D Decision Advisor: An interactive approach to normative decision system model construction", European Journal of Operational Research, Vol. 84:1, pp. 116-133, 1995.

34. Mintzberg H., Raisinghani D., Theoret A., "The structure of' unstructured" decision processes", Administrative Science Quarterly, Vol. 21 (2), pp. 246-275, 1976.

35. Sahar Karimi., "A purchase decision-making process model of online consumers and its influential factor a cross sector analysis", 2013.

36. Smith A. D., Rupp W. T., "Strategic online customer decision making: leveraging the transformational power of the Internet", Online Information Review, Vol. 27 (6), pp. 418-432, 2003.

37. Lee Y., Kozar K. A., "Investigating the effect of website quality on e-business success: An analytic hierarchy process (AHP) approach", Decision Support Systems, Vol. 42, pp. 1383-1401, 2006, doi:10.1016/j. dss.2005.11.005.

38. Darley W. K., Blankson, C., Luethge, D. J., "Toward an integrated framework for online consumer behavior and decision making process: A review", Psychology and Marketing, Vol. 27 (2), pp. 94-116, 2010.

39. Shang R-A., Chen Y., Shen C., Lysander., "Extrinsic versus intrinsic motivations for consumers to shop on-line", Information & Management, Vol. 42, pp. 401-413, 2005 doi:10.1016/j.im.2004.01.009.

40. Coker B. L. S., Ashill N. J., Hope B., "Measuring internet product purchase risk", European Journal of Marketing, Vol. 45 (7), pp. 1130-1151, 2011, doi:10.1108/03090561111137642.

41. Koufaris M., "Applying the technology acceptance model and flow theory to online consumer behavior", Information Systems Research, Vol. 13 (2), pp. 205-223, 2002, doi:10.1287/isre.13.2.205.83.

42. Dejan P., "Analysis of consumer behavior online", 2007, Retrieved November 24, 2010, from http:// analogik.com/articles/227/analysis-of-consumer-behaviour-online.

43. Koiso-Kanttila N., "Time, attention, authenticity and consumer benefits of the web", Business Horizons, Vol. 48, pp. 63-70, 2005, doi:10.1016/j.bushor.2004.10.004.

44. Kurnia S., Schubert P., "Toward achieving customer satisfaction in online grocery shopping", Electronic Customer Relationship Management, pp. 177-196, 2006.

45. Seock Y. K., Norton J. T., "Capturing college students on the web: Analysis of clothing web site attributes", Journal of Fashion Marketing and Management, Vol. 11 (4), pp. 539-552, 2007.

46. Dholakia U. M., Rego L. L.,"What makes commercial web page popular: an empirical study of online shopping", In Proceedings of 32nd Hawaii International Conference on System Sciences, New York, NY: Institute of Electrical and Electronics Engineers, pp. 5-8, 1998

47. Goslar, M.D. and Brown, S.W., "Decision support systems: advantages in consumer marketing settings", The Journal of Consumer Marketing, Vol. 3 No. 3, Summer 1986, pp. 43-50.

48. Knuckles, B.M., "New techniques and changes in research design – their impacts on the brand and advertising development process", Journal of Advertising Research, Vol. 26 No. 3, April-May 1986, pp. RC6-9.

49. Wierenga, B., "The first generation of marketing expert systems", Working Study Series, No. 90-009, Marketing Department, The Wharton School, University of Pennsylvania, Philadelphia, PA, 1990.

50. Davenport, T.H. and Short, J.E., "The new industrial engineering: information technology and business process redesign", Sloan Management Review, Vol. 31 No. 4, summer 1990, pp. 11-27.

51. Fletcher, K., Buttery, A. and Deans, K., "A structure and content of the marketing information system: a guide for management", Marketing Intelligence and Planning, Vol. 6 No. 4, 1988, pp. 27-35.

52. Sääksjärvi, M.V.T. and Talvinen, J.M., "Integration and effectiveness of marketing information systems", European Journal of Marketing, Vol. 27 No. 1, 1993, pp. 64-79

53. Martell, D., "Marketing and information technology", European Journal of Marketing, Vol. 22 No. 9, 1988, pp. 16- 24.

54. Rangaswamy, A. and Wind, Y., "Information technology in marketing", in Kent, A. and Williams, J.G. (Eds), Encyclopaedia of Microcomputers, Vol. 9, Marcel Dekker Inc., New York, NY, November 1991, pp. 67-83.

55. Neha Jain (2014), E-Marketing and the consumer decision making process, synopsis for the degree of doctor of philosophy in management, Jaypee institute of information technology, Noida

56. Becker, Gary S. (1976), "A Theory of the Allocation of Time," The Economic Approach to Human Behavior, G. S. Becker. ed.. Chicago: University of California Press.

57. Berk, Richard A. (1980), "The New Home Economics: An Agenda for Sociological Research," Women and Household Labor, S. F. Berk, ed., Beverly Hills, CA: Sage.

58. Davis, Harry L. (1976), "Decision Making Within the Household." Journal of Consumer Research, 1, 51-62.

59. Douglas, Mary and Baron Isherwood (1979), The World of Goods, New York: Basic Books.

60. Etgar, Michael (1978), "The Household as a Production Unit," Research in Marketing, J. N. Sheth, ed., 1, JA Press.

61. Feldman, Laurance P. and Jacob Hornik (1981), "The Use of Time: An Integrated Conceptual Model," Journal of Consumer Research, 7 (4), 407-419.

62. Ferber, Robert and Lucy Chao Lee, "Husband-Wife Influence in Family Purchasing Buyer," Journal of Consumer Research, 1, 43-50.

63. Firat, A. Fuat and Nikhilesh Dholakia (1982), "Consumption Choices at the Macro Level," Journal of Macro- marketing, 2 (Fall 2), 6-15.

64. Fried, J. and P. Molnar (1975), "General Model for Culture and Technology," in Technological Forecasting and Social Change, 8 (2), 175-188.

65. Hendrix, Philip E., Thomas C. Kinnear, and James R. Taylor (1979), "The Allocation of Time by Consumers," Advances in Consumer Research, 7, 35-40.

66. Hendrix, Philip E. (1984), "Antecedents and Consequences of Time Use: Proposed Measures and Preliminary Evidence," Advances in Consumer Research, 11, 35-40.

67. Houthakker, H. S. (1960), "The Influence of Prices and Incomes on Household Expenditures," Bulletin of Inter- national Institute of Statistics, 37.

68. Michelson, William (1980), "Spatial and Temporal Dimensions of Child Care," SIGNS, 5 (3), 542-547.

69. Morgan, J., I. Sirageldin, and N. Baerwaldt (1966), Productive Americans, Ann Arbor, MI: Institute for Social Research.

70. Moschis, George P., Thomas Stanley, and Jac L. Goldstucker (1983), "Will Consumer Acceptance of Videotex Services Affect Marketing," working study, Georgia State University .

71. Nicosia, Franco (1983), "Consumers, Information, and Structural Changes in the Family," study presented at the ACR Conference.

72. Parsons, T. (1951), Toward a General Theory of Action, Cambridge: Harvard University Press.

73. Reilly, Michael d. (1982), "Working Wives and Convenience Consumption," Journal of Consumer Research, 8 (4), 407-418.

74. Roberts, Mary Lou and L. Wortzel (forthcoming), Changing Household, Boston: Ballinger Company.

75. Robinson, J., P. Converse, and A. Szalai (1972), "Everyday Life in the Twelve Countries," in A. Szalai et al., The Use of Time. The Hague: Mouton Press.

76. Strober, Myra H. and Charles B. Weinberg (1977), "Working Wives and Major Family Expenditures," Journal of Consumer Research, 4 (3), 141-147.

77. Szalai, A. (1972), The Use of Time, The Hague: Mouton Press.

78. Thrall, Charles A. (1982), "The Conservative Use of Modern Household Technology," Technology and Culture, 23 (2). 175-194.

79. TIME (1983), "Machine of the Year," (Computers), (January 3), 12-39.

80. Tydeman, John (1982), "Videotex: Ushering in the Electronic Household," Futurist, 16 (1 February), 54-61.

81. Vanek, Joann (1978), "Household Technology and Social Status: Rising Living Standards and Status and Residence Differences in Housework," Technology and Culture, 19. 361-365.

82. Venkatesh, A. and N. Vitalari (Forthcoming), "Households and Technology: The Case of Home.Computers- Some Theoretical Issues," in M. L. Roberts and L. Wortzel, Changing Household, Ballinger Publishing Co.

83. Venkatesh, A. and N. Vitalari (1983), "An Empirical Study of Home Computer Adoption and Usage," working study, University of California, Irvine.

84. Walker (1969), "Homemaking Still Takes Time," Journal of Home Economics, 61 (October), 621-624.

85. Wortzel, Lawrence H. (1980), 'Marital Roles and Typologies as Predictors of Purchase Decision Making for Everyday Household Products: Suggestions for Research," Advances in Consumer Research, 212-216.

**Website:**

• http://smallbusiness.chron.com/advantages-information-technology-business-774.html

• https://www.cdnsol.com/blog/how-it-can-contribute-in-fmcg-industry

• https://www.business2community.com/tech-gadgets/importance-information-technology-business-today-01393380

• https://jobs.lovetoknow.com/how-is-information-technology-used-marketing-careers

• https://www.useoftechnology.com/technology-marketing/

• http://www.kimtasso.com/faq/what-is-the-impact-of-technology-on-marketing/

- https://bizfluent.com/info-7747420-use-computer-technology-marketing.html
- https://www.tisindia.com/blog/5-reasons-why-internet-marketing-is-important-for-your-business/
- https://www.digitalvidya.com/blog/growth-of-digital-marketing-industry-in-india/
- https://www.wordstream.com/web-marketing
- http://www.acrwebsite.org/volumes/6382/volumes/v12/NA-12
- http://marketing-interface.com/digital-tools/marketing-technology-every-organization-needs/
- http://smallbusiness.chron.com/technology-marketing-products-3307.html